Political Communication

T0333229

Books in the Politics Study Guides series

Political Communication

Steven Foster

Edinburgh University Press

Edinburgh University Press Ltd
22 George Square, Edinburgh
www.euppublishing.com

Typeset in 11/13pt Monotype Baskerville by
Servis Filmsetting Ltd, Stockport, Cheshire, and
printed and bound in Great Britain by
CPI Antony Rowe, Chippenham and Eastbourne

A CIP record for this book is available from the British Library

ISBN 978 0 7486 2571 0 (paperback)

The right of Steven Foster to be identified as author of
this work has been asserted in accordance with the
Copyright, Designs and Patents Act 1988.

Published with the support of the Edinburgh University Scholarly
Publishing Initiatives Fund.

Contents

Boxes

Tables

Preface

The purpose of this book became clear when I finally settled on a title. Though it doesn't say much about my skills as a writer, completing this seemingly simple task had proved elusive. At first, I had been minded to persuade the Series Editor and the staff at Edinburgh University Press to abandon the working title and instead publish it as *The Politics of the Media*. Yet upon further reflection I felt that a specific reference to the media would obscure what it was I was really trying to achieve. This is not to say that the media does not figure prominently in what follows. However, 'political communication' – a more complex and expansive concept – encapsulates more accurately the book's main subject. This addresses the way in which politicians attempt to communicate their messages to an increasingly sceptical and disengaged electorate and the implications this has for a wide range of associated issues: their relations with journalists, our understanding of media bias and effects, government policy on media ownership and content, and so on.

Nor can the topicality of political communication be seriously questioned. Anyone with the slightest interest in UK politics over the last decade will be aware that political communication has become one of the defining issues of the era. To repackage Marshall McLuhan's famous dictum: the medium has once again become the message. The communication strategy adopted by Tony Blair's Labour party has played the key part in this process. Blair and his team showed the UK just how sophisticated a modern political communications strategy can become. Subsequent changes to the very language of politics tell their own tale. If few of us had heard of them before, it was not long before the terms 'spin doctor' and, more simply, 'spin' entered everyday usage. In the process, some of its most celebrated practitioners – Peter Mandelson, Charlie Whelan, Jo Moore and, most especially, Alastair Campbell – became some of the most talked about political actors in the UK.

However, towards the end of the Blair era, these terms had taken on a more serious connotation. In the aftermath of the invasion of Iraq and the tragic death of Dr David Kelly, Blair ended his premiership mired in a controversy which extended beyond questions of his personal integrity and on to the constitutional propriety of the large communications operation that followed him into office. There is, of course, a strange irony in this. Despite the accusations that he routinely and successfully manipulated journalists in a bid to gain short-term political advantage, by the time he left office his relationship with large sections of the media had broken down. It was wholly fitting, therefore, that his final keynote speech sought to initiate a debate on what he considered to be the near impossibility of conducting open and serious political discourse in the face of an unscrupulous, market-driven and 'feral' media beast. There was a tacit acknowledgment in all this that Blair and his communication strategists may have contributed to their own problems. At the same time, he left his audience in no doubt that he, Campbell and the others were much more sinned against than sinning. Consequently, three years after his resignation as prime minister, this might be a timely moment to consider the nature of contemporary political communication and, more importantly, the role it plays in the conduct of British politics in the first decade of the twenty-first century.

As is so often the case when a book is published – in this respect, at least, this author is no different from any other – there are many whose support and encouragement must be acknowledged. Firstly, I should once again like to thank my old friend and series editor, Duncan Watts, for his guidance and tolerance, hoping that he finds in this work at least one or two items that bear favourable comparison with his own. Secondly, Nicola Ramsey, James Dale and their colleagues at Edinburgh University Press have once again shown seemingly limitless forbearance and the highest standards of professionalism in making good my deficiencies. Thirdly, despite the unexpected twists and turns in my teaching career, I am ever mindful of the continuous debt I owe to my colleagues in the Politics Department at the Manchester Grammar School. The Department and indeed the wider community of the Manchester Grammar School was rocked by the sudden and most untimely death of its founding head, Dr Rod Martin, which occurred whilst this book was nearing completion. It is only fitting, therefore, that I take this opportunity to record Rod's remarkable contribution to the life of the school and, beyond that, to political education across the UK. It is something of an understatement to add that he played a pivotal role in the development of my own career and that he will be most sorely missed.

Further, and on a different note, Lynn and Kathryn have suffered much in the making of what the latter (ominously from the point of view of future sales) describes as 'this boring book'. Perhaps one or both of them might eventually decide that their relative deprivation was worthwhile. Finally, the older I get, clearer still becomes the debt I owe my parents. Consequently, it is to my mother and the memory of my late father that this book is dedicated.

SF
Bramhall, Cheshire
September 2009

Introduction

Whilst all of this book has in some way been influenced by its central theme (how politicians seek to communicate their political messages), its content has been divided into three quite distinctive parts. The first of these examines political communication from the perspective of parties competing to win elections. It focuses, in other words, on how parties organise their internal communications in order to realise their political goals. With this in mind, I do not think I am overstretching the bounds of literary convention by opening with a chapter that sets party political communication in its proper historical context. Chapter 1 duly maps the main changes that have occurred since 1918, whilst also seeking to identify the combination of 'push' and 'pull' factors that helped to bring them about.

Chapters 2 to 4 build on these foundations by examining some of the key features of party political communication. There is an element of selection in this. Nonetheless, I am confident that my choice of subject matter will provide the reader with at least some insight into the complex nature of modern political communication. Chapter 2 kicks off this process by studying the way in which political communication is subject to extensive strategic planning. It focuses in particular on the way in which this strategic dimension depends upon private opinion research and highly centralised campaign management. Chapter 3 fulfils a similar function in respect of constituency campaigning in the digital age, whilst Chapter 4 examines the main elements of what Dominic Wring has called the controlled elements of political marketing: party broadcasts and political advertising. Chapter 5 returns to the main theme by exploring the techniques deployed by politicians in their bid to influence the all-important news agenda. Inevitably, this chapter focuses heavily on the work of press and publicity officers (a somewhat austere description of spin doctors) and the sophisticated systems of rebuttal and news management they have put in place. In this way, Chapter 5 sets the scene for Chapter 6, which looks at the way in which these techniques were incorporated into government communication after 1997. This aspect of the Blair years has given rise to considerable comment. Consequently, Chapter 6 will review these developments and hopefully shed a little light on why they are mired in so much controversy.

In the course of this analysis it will become quite clear to the reader that the dominant trend within what we might call party political communication is media management. So important are mediated communications, the process by which parties communicate to voters through the media, that it is quite impossible to conceive of political communication outside the nexus linking politician and journalist. This explains the nature of the second part of the book. Here, I set out to explore in more detail why politicians put so much effort into managing the media, something which draws out a discussion of those two perennially important issues: media bias and media influence. The first of these is examined in Chapter 7, the second in Chapter 8.

The third and final part of the book takes the relationship between politicians and media one stage further by examining government media policy. In particular, it seeks to identify the extent to which, given that media management is so fundamental to political communication, government has manipulated the law on ownership and media content to its advantage. Chapter 9 looks at the law on ownership, whilst Chapter 10 completes the book with an examination of the complementary issue of content regulation.

I can make no claim that this study provides an original, leave alone a definitive, account of a complex and fascinating area of contemporary politics. I have had to be highly selective in my final choice of material and am only too aware that the book is open to a number of criticisms on this count alone. In particular, I have largely neglected political communication outside the party political arena, whilst, within it, I have devoted disproportionate attention to the major parties. At the same time, I have done my utmost to remain true to the central aim of the Political Study Guides series and produce a volume that presents the more ambitious student (and the interested general reader happily freed from the constraints of exam preparation) with a challenging introduction. I can only hope that my efforts have not been wholly in vain.

CHAPTER 1

Party Political Communication in Historical Perspective

Contents

Overview

This chapter charts the recent history of party political communication in the UK. It seeks to map the key changes and explain why some analysts have organised these into three successive phases: pre-modern, modern and post-modern. In this way, it serves as a preview for the more detailed analyses which follow over the next five chapters.

Key issues to be covered in this chapter

- The distinguishing features of the pre-modern and modern eras
- The factors which explain the emergence of the modern
- The uneven nature of change during this period of transition
- The post-modern thesis and its implications for our understanding of current trends in party political communication

Pre-modern to modern

The concept of party political communication is defined by its relationship to voters and voting behaviour. As Denver (2007: 125) notes, communicating with voters in the hope of influencing their behaviour is as old as competitive politics itself: 'For as long as there have been contested elections . . . those standing for election and their supporters have endeavoured . . . to persuade the relevant electorate to vote for them.' It follows that, as elections became more competitive, politicians sought more efficient means of communicating their messages. This was especially so during the late nineteenth and early twentieth centuries, when franchise reform created a much larger and socially diverse electorate. In turn, this triggered a wide-ranging and imaginative response, most notably from the Conservative party (Crockett 1994).

However, despite the upsurge in interest in political communication after World War I, Norris (1997) still prefers to describe this period as 'pre-modern' (see Box 1.1), an era which survived more or less intact until the late 1950s. More than that of any other individual, it is the career of **Harold Macmillan** which marks the transition to a distinctively modern era of political communication. When Macmillan assumed the premiership on 10 January 1957, his political inheritance was decidedly gloomy. In the aftermath of the **Suez crisis**, support for the Conservatives had plummeted, leaving Labour confident of overturning their 68-seat deficit whenever a general election was called. In the event, however, Macmillan easily saw off Labour's challenge. More importantly, he did so using techniques that suggested that party political communication had jettisoned the old methods (Rosenbaum 1997: 5–8; Wring 2005: 48–50).

The main features of the modern era are described in some detail in Box 1.2. One particularly striking break with the past was the emergence of distinctly national campaigning. This suggested that political communication had become too important to be left in the hands of individual candidates and their bands of local volunteers. This also explains some of the other defining features of the modern era such as the growing prominence of marketing professionals, private opinion research and national advertising.

Box 1.1 The defining characteristics of the pre-modern era

Retail politics
Communication was largely undertaken by small armies of willing volunteers seeking direct contact with voters in a bid to 'sell' their parties' candidates. Political advertising was notably under-utilised.

Limited central coordination
Overarching communication strategies and centralised campaign management were conspicuous only by their absence.

The relative absence of communication professionals
Politicians were confident in their own abilities to understand the electoral 'mood'. Consequently, marketing and public relations (PR) also played limited parts in the communications process.

Non-mediated communication
Little thought was given to the needs of the media who, where this was permitted, were expected to report politicians' speeches more or less verbatim.

A narrow time-frame
Communications focused on the three- to four-week 'official' campaign. There was no sense that campaigning should be extended over a longer period, leave alone that it should become a permanent feature of day-to-day politics.

However, the single most important change concerned the means by which campaign messages were communicated. The pre-modern era was quintessentially the era of retail politics, where parties were 'sold' on doorsteps and in meeting rooms up and down the country. By contrast, in the modern era parties increasingly designed their communications around the needs of the print and especially the broadcast media. Rather than focusing their efforts on communicating directly with voters, instead they preferred to channel their messages via journalists, the loss of editorial control being compensated for by better and more efficient access.

Box 1.2 Modern political communication

The strategic dimension
Modern political communication has a strong strategic element. This is devised by national campaign teams and is invariably built around the characteristics of individual party leaders.

Professionalisation
Large teams of professional advisors are *sine qua non* for modern communication. Their presence is felt throughout the campaign, but especially in political advertising and media management.

The long campaign
Modern communication strategies commence some time in advance of the official campaign. One reason for this is the important strategic goal of setting a favourable media agenda.

Opinion research and marketing
Communication strategies exploit modern marketing techniques, especially opinion research. Above all, these are designed to encourage target voters to associate a party with certain qualities, for example reasonableness, integrity and competence.

National advertising
This is prominent and carefully designed to reinforce the central campaign messages. Adverts do not advocate policies but are instead heavily image-based and shaped around simple slogans.

Mediated communications
Modern communication is highly attuned to the needs of the media, especially television. The goal of press and publicity officers ('spin doctors') is to set the media's agenda, ensuring that the headlines are dominated by stories which play to their party's advantage.

Explaining the transition: 'push' and 'pull' factors

This transformation was the result of a combination of 'push' and 'pull' factors. The former undermined the viability of pre-modern communications; the latter reinforced this by giving campaign managers positive reasons for change.

Table 1.1 Party identification: 1964–2005 (figures as percentage of the electorate)					
Strength of identification	**1964**	**February 1974**	**1983**	**1992**	**2005**
Very strong	44	30	22	18	8
Fairly strong	40	43	41	45	37
Not very strong	11	18	24	27	36
Expressing some identification	95	91	87	80	81
Expressing no identification	5	9	13	20	19

(*Source:* Allen 2006: 58)

Dealignment

Perhaps the decisive push factor was the emergence of a dealigned electorate. Pre-modern campaigners had made a number of assumptions about voters and their behaviour. This was encapsulated in the concept of party identification, described by Denver (2007: 84) as a sea anchor tying voters to 'their' parties for life. **Dealignment** challenged these assumptions by insisting that the 'anchor' had worked itself loose, the implication being that 'voters are likely to be more open to persuasion, more indecisive about which party to vote for and more likely to switch parties' (2007: 84).

Further, dealignment pointed to an array of other important social and cultural changes, including widespread disengagement from mainstream ideologies and an 'anti-party' **Zeitgeist**, in which party propaganda was invariably met with cynical disbelief (Lees-Marshment 2001: 22–4). Communicating with the electorate in such circumstances presented parties with challenges on a scale not seen since World War I. Most importantly, it no longer seemed credible to mount a retail campaign based on historic beliefs and aimed more or less exclusively at traditional voting groups. Indeed, on the last occasion a major party attempted this (Labour in June 1983), it suffered its worst defeat for half a century.

Table 1.2 Electoral volatility: 1964–2001 (figures as percentage of the electorate)

General election	Switched parties	Made final choice during the campaign	Considered voting for another party
1964	18	12	25
1966	10	11	23
1970	16	12	21
Average: 1964–70	**14.7**	**11.7**	**23.0**
February 1974	24	23	25
October 1974	16	22	21
1979	22	28	31
1983	23	22	25
1987	19	24	28
1992	19	24	26
1997	25	27	31
2001	22	26	not available
2005	25	33	not available
Average: 1974–2005	**21.7**	**25.4**	**26.7**

(*Source:* Denver 2007: 87, 90)

Equally, however, dealignment was not all bad news. Prior to 1970, there seemed little incentive in trying to persuade wide sections of a largely stable electorate to change their views. Thereafter, in an age when as many as one in four voters routinely switched allegiance, parties had every reason to seek out new groups of supporters. Margaret Thatcher understood this quicker than most, which was one reason why her Conservative party trounced Labour so thoroughly in the years between 1979 and 1987.

The eclipse of the activist-ideological party
The effects of dealignment were compounded by the dramatic reduction in the capacity of constituency parties to mount meaningful

Table 1.3 Party membership: 1987–2005			
Year	Conservatives (000s)	Labour (000s)	Liberal Democrats (000s)
1987	1,000	289	138
1992	500	280	100
1997	400	405	100
2001	350	311	90
2005	320	215	73

(*Source:* Allen 2006: 66)

campaigns at that level. One reason for this was long-term decline in the number of people joining their local parties. By the mid-1970s, the Conservatives had lost over half their post-war membership, Labour a third – since when the general trend has continued downwards. Further, relatively few of those members who remain are likely to be 'active'. In 2005, for example, it was estimated that, with 70,000 voters in an average constituency, candidates typically had 42 campaign workers at their disposal prior to polling day (Fisher et al. 2005: 6–7). The limitations this placed on local campaigning can be all too easily guessed at, the chief casualty being the tradition of mass canvassing. Since local parties lacked the capacity to persuade voters, canvassers simply used contacts to record their voting intentions.

Yet, whilst the lost membership was no doubt regretted, it is doubtful whether national campaign managers would have continued to trust local volunteers even where the latter retained a strategic campaigning capacity. This is so because the era of dealignment coincided with the collapse of historic ideological divisions between the main parties, with the result that elections now turn largely on competing claims of managerial competence. Communicating the latter is not easy. In particular, it draws heavily on both the latest marketing techniques and the media, something which places a huge premium on presentation and demands a very different set of skills to those held by local volunteers.

Box 1.3 The Political Parties, Elections and Referendums Act 2000

In the aftermath of the 1997 general election, a chorus of opinion demanded that national campaign expenditure be properly regulated. The result was the Political Parties, Elections and Referendums Act 2000 (PPERA), which duly placed a cap on the campaign expenditure of party headquarters. In the year before a general election (the regulated period falls to four months for other contests), no party can spend more than £30,000 for each constituency contested, up to a maximum of £18.84 million in Great Britain and £540,000 in Northern Ireland.

The law and party funding

Happily for the parties, developments elsewhere 'pulled' them towards a new mode of communication just when the latter was most needed. This process originated in an important clarification of electoral law. Until 1952, it was believed to be unlawful for national party organisations to spend money on political communication *once a campaign had formally begun*. This belief, combined with the tight statutory controls on constituency campaign expenditure, had seriously hampered the development of expansive communications strategies. In 1952, however, the case of *R* v. ***Tronah Mines*** established the principle that national party organisations could indeed promote their own campaigns without committing any offence. Party headquarters were now free to spend what they liked both before and during election campaigns, providing of course they could first raise the money

It took the main parties until February 1974 to fully appreciate the implications of *Tronah Mines*. However, after this point they consistently demonstrated the ability to accumulate considerable campaign 'war chests', albeit at the risk of their long-term financial health to say nothing of their integrity. By 1997, the fundraisers had done their work so well that Parliament voted to place the first statutory limits on national campaign expenditure (Box 1.3). All the same, it cannot be credibly argued that a 'ceiling' of £18 million will seriously compromise the tradition of ambitious national campaigning.

Table 1.4 The growth of expenditure by party headquarters (selected general elections)

Year	Conservative (£)	Labour (£)
1950	135,000	84,000
1959	631,000	239,000
1970	630,000	526,000
1979	2,333,000	1,566,000
1992	11,196,000	10,597,000
2005	17, 859,000	17,940,000

(*Source:* Butler 1995: 86; Electoral Commission)

Political television: the road from Rochdale

National campaign budgets of this scale have been used to finance the exercises in marketing, advertising and above all public relations, which together have redefined the nature of party political communication. In turn, these developments are rooted in the revolution in broadcasting-content regulations which finally permitted television and radio journalists to report elections as they were happening. Before the mid-1950s, broadcasters were prevented from the contemporaneous coverage of election contests. This prohibition was strongly associated with **Lord Reith**. Yet, like so many other aspects of his legacy, it did not long survive the arrival of commercial television in 1955. The first indication of this was the 1958 Rochdale by-election. Granada Television, which held the local ITV franchise, decided to broadcast two candidate debates together with the count. Not wishing to be outdone, the BBC broadcast interviews with a number of voters. The result of the contest – a Labour gain at the expense of the Conservatives – was far less important than the fact that legal action was not taken against the television producers, effectively giving them a 'green light' to extensively cover the general election held eighteen months or so later. UK politicians could now entertain the prospect of following their North American counterparts and re-route their political messages via this most powerful medium.

Box 1.4 The power of television

Efficiency
Television scores heavily in what Negrine (1994: 154) calls its 'immediacy and universality'. The overwhelming majority of voters can access television sets and are exposed to a remarkable amount of political coverage as a consequence.

Psychology
Television is a visual medium and research tells us that images are much more compelling than the spoken word. To cite but one recent study: 53 per cent of respondents were influenced most by image; 32 per cent by how they were addressed; and a mere 7 per cent by what was said to them (Jones 2006: 224, 226). Moving images are more compelling still. With a sound bite that could form the opening to a spin doctor's manual, Rosenbaum concludes that 'A picture is worth a thousand words, but a moving picture is worth ten thousand' (1997: 81).

Compatibility with the Zeitgeist
Voter attitudes are seemingly shaped by a range of cultural constraints, including: a shorter attention span; a reluctance to consider issues in depth; and a greater capacity to absorb information quickly. Politicians know they have at most 20 seconds to make a significant impact. However, providing they link powerful images to a memorable phrase or sound bite, even 20 seconds of exposure on television offers a greater capacity to reach target voters than any other medium.

Enhanced ability to shape the political agenda
Whilst there remains considerable debate over the ability of television to tell voters what to think, it has an obvious potential to tell them what to think about. Television has thus moved into the vacuum created by the decline of alternative sources of opinion: community leaders, religious organisations and trade unions.

Perceptions of impartiality
Television is widely accepted by the electorate as impartial and hence trustworthy.

Cost-effectiveness
Communication mediated via television remains far cheaper than other forms of campaigning, especially political advertising.

The North American analogy is important, since it is the USA which provides the first major example of television's power. On 23 September 1952, Republican vice-presidential candidate Richard Nixon used television to address directly 60 million US voters, accompanied by one of the most famous props in television history: a small dog named Checkers. Accused of campaign finance abuses, Nixon was in deep political trouble. However, rather than rebut the charges directly, Nixon wrong-footed his opponents by appearing to 'confess' on air that his family had indeed received gifts from well-wishers, including the aforementioned Checkers. Nixon then defiantly stated that, whatever his opponents might say, he would be keeping the dog. Checkers, or so it would seem, had stolen the hearts of his young daughters; the implication being that Nixon would risk political ruin rather than upset his children. With the small dog now almost symbolising his integrity, Nixon effectively asked a simple yet unanswerable question: how could such a man, a loving and self-sacrificing parent, be guilty of the things that 'they' are accusing him of?

At a stroke – and a master one at that – Nixon demonstrated some of the fundamental truths about televisual communication: speak to viewers as one individual to another; avoid drawn out explanations; use imagery rather than words; and above all, rehearse and revise your techniques. In the years which followed, analyses of political communication soon took for granted TV's unrivalled communicative power (Negrine 1994: 154). New generations of politicians responded by spending small fortunes on securing the skills of media advisers and public relations 'gurus'. Jones (2006: 224) captures their mindset when he writes that: 'Two minutes of exposure on peak time television enables politicians to reach more people than they could in a lifetime of canvassing, handshaking or addressing public meetings.' The task facing parties was to provide television producers with the material they required for their programming and in this way steer the political agenda in the desired direction.

Uneven development

It would, however, be a mistake to imagine that the emergence of the modern era was an even and consistent process. Complacency played a part in this. After their 1959 success the Conservatives erroneously concluded they had mastered the new techniques and duly allowed the initiative to pass to Labour. This pattern then repeated itself, but in reverse order; its triumphs in 1964 and again in 1966 having a similarly soporific effect on Labour. The Conservatives, meanwhile, overhauled their campaign organisation and set about constructing the strategy which restored them to power in 1970.

Equally, however, modernisation was hampered by internal opposition. This was most famously so in the case of the Labour party between 1970 and 1994 (Gould 1988). In his account of the emergence of New Labour, **Philip Gould** points out that he had been commissioned by Peter Mandelson as early as 1985 to find out why so many working-class voters had abandoned the party. However, despite the positive reception his work received from Mandelson and the then Labour leader, Neil Kinnock, Gould doubts whether his findings were ever properly incorporated into the party's communications strategies for the 1987 and 1992 general elections. Further, such was the subsequent reaction against the modernisers under the leadership of John Smith (1992–4) that Gould left the UK to work for Bill Clinton's campaign team in Little Rock, Arkansas. On his return, he produced another internal paper – *1992 Campaign Evaluation and Implications* – on how Labour might benefit from the strategy and techniques adopted by the Clinton team. This was followed by a public piece co-authored with Patricia Hewitt and published in *Renewal* in January 1993. However, once again his report, along with a raft of memos written over the months which followed, met with considerable internal opposition. It was only after Smith's death in May 1994 and Blair's election that his particular view of political communication with its emphasis on marketing and opinion research was finally welcomed.

As a result, party political communication has tended to evolve in 'fits and starts'. Invariably, it has had to await the emergence (and re-emergence) of leaders both willing to follow expert advice and sufficiently powerful to face down internal critics, the careers of Margaret Thatcher and Tony Blair being particularly important in this respect (Lees-Marshment 2001).

At the same time, one should not forget that political communication is an art, not a science. Consequently, an understanding

---

Box 1.5 An uneasy transition: internal party resistance to modern political communication

Politicians' vanity
Politicians pride themselves on their ability to understand voters and resent suggestions that they need help from people used to marketing soap powder and other workaday products.

Dilution of values and tradition
The findings of marketing professionals often make for uncomfortable reading. Invariably, they advocate policy, organisational and presentational changes at the expense of historic values and traditions.

The role of political parties
Some politicians – **Tony Benn** being a particularly notable example – believe that parties must offer distinctive choices. This runs counter to the advice of communication experts, who focus on the optimum means of selling the party to as many voters as possible.

Leadership control
Modern communication concentrates power in the hands of the leader. Others may resist this by promoting traditional mechanisms for encouraging participation and leadership accountability.

Empirical evidence
When parties suffer unexpected electoral defeats, they often turn on their professional advisers. This was true of the Conservatives in 1964 and Labour in both 1970 and 1979.

---

of the main techniques is only acquired over time, new ideas being introduced, dropped and refined with each contest. Political advertising provides one example of this. Though the Conservatives' use of advertising in 1959 was revolutionary (text was radically reduced whilst photographs of politicians disappeared altogether), the actual messages were still positive. Twenty years later and now under the influence of Saatchi and Saatchi, the same party swept to power on the back of the most sustained *negative* advertising campaign UK politics had yet seen. Thereafter, with one or two exceptions, advertising has moved relentlessly in this direction.

Media management presents a similar picture. Whilst the use of the sound bite was pioneered by Harold Wilson in 1963–4, it was not until the 1979 general election that its close cousin, the photo opportunity (or 'photo-op'), became the dominant feature of public relations. Thereafter, as Margaret Thatcher's campaign manager Gordon Reece had predicted, the power of physical images became so compelling that they have come to dominate political communication to a point where it is suggested that party leaders are routinely chosen because of their telegenic qualities.

The costs of campaigning

So far, discussion has focused on the uneven nature of change *within* parties. Arguably, however, it is the unevenness of change *between* parties that is much more significant. Finance holds the key to this. Until recently, the Labour and Conservative parties alone demonstrated the capacity to raise the income needed to deploy consistently the full range of modern communication techniques. (The one exception to this was the Referendum party in the 1997 general election. Backed by the late Sir James Goldsmith, it was able to spend unprecedented amounts for a minor party.) Notwithstanding the inherent reasonableness of allowing private individuals to finance their preferred political causes, the data in Table 1.5 are hardly an advertisement for the equitable nature of British democracy. As a result, the majority of parties only buy into the modern as much as their finances and to a lesser extent their ideologies allow. This creates an important caveat, which the reader is urged to bear in mind throughout the remainder of this study.

Targeting and niche marketing: a post-modern paradigm?

Over the last two decades party political communication has continued to evolve rapidly, so much so that it is now suggested that a new, post-modern era is coming into being (Norris 1997). Post-modernism was used by **critical theorists** to support their contention that the major political ideologies – conservatism, socialism, liberalism – had lost their hold on the public consciousness. This has numerous implications for party political communication.

Table 1.5 Selected items of campaign expenditure in the 2001 and 2005 general elections

Party (year)	Party political broadcasts (£)	Advertising (£)	Unsolicited materials (£)	Market research (£)	Media manage-ment (£)	Rallies (£)	Total
Conservatives (2001)	567,286	4,409,569	1,216,770	1,717,093	356,639	1,972,362	12,751,813
Conservatives (2005)	293,446	8,175,166	4,493,021	1,291,847	448,277	1,148,218	17,854,241
Labour (2001)	272,849	5,024,259	1,451,778	869,338	750,395	1,283,721	10,945,119
Labour (2005)	470,218	5,286,997	2,698,114	1,577,017	375,410	2,916,969	17,939,617
Lib Dems (2001)	55,353	196,595	54,287	66,016	230,787	73,917	1,361,372
Lib Dems (2005)	124,871	1,583,058	1,235,295	165,185	105,793	68,994	4,234,574
SNP (2001)	38,794	51,723	65,127	2,971	38,551	5,597	226,203
SNP (2005)	41,607	40,411	30,165	26,090	28,398	–	193,387
Greens (2001)	21,545	984	1,963	–	3,181	–	44,912
Greens (2005)	15,944	106,738	27,179	–	694	947	160,224
BNP (2001)	–	–	–	–	–	–	–
BNP (2005)	3,173	235	106,303	–	900	78	112,068

(Source: Electoral Commission)

- Firstly, it suggests that electoral behaviour is likely to become even more volatile and still harder to predict. Recent trends in the spatial dimension of general election results, most notably the collapse of uniform swings, already offer supporting evidence of this (Curtice and Steed 1997: 298; King 2006).
- Secondly, it hints at increasing fragmentation within the electorate, something that necessarily lends itself to carefully targeted and personalised campaigning. This applies both to content and form. The internet, to cite but one example, has created unprecedented opportunities for individuals to determine their own sources of news, especially when used in conjunction with other aspects of digital communication such as the mobile telephone.
- Thirdly, it encourages the belief that new generations of voters – the so-called 'digital natives' – cannot be reached through the traditional means of modern communication: mass political advertising and broadcast communications.

The key developments can be seen in Box 1.6. Of these, Norris (1997: 77, 87) regards the fragmentation of communications and the

Box 1.6 Selected features of the post-modern paradigm

Decentralisation
Whilst the overarching communication strategy has retained its dominance, the management of much campaigning has been decentralised in order to give it greater sensitivity to local realities. Ironically, this has led to a revival in constituency campaigning albeit in a new form.

Targeting and niche marketing
The national campaign is largely composed of a series of closely contested local battles. Parties now deploy the widest range of targeting and niche marketing strategies to win these 'battleground' seats. Elsewhere, so-called safe seats are scarcely contested.

Further professionalisation
Decentralisation, targeting and niche marketing are impossible without the full deployment of campaign professionals, who operate independently of traditional party structures.

Permanent campaigning
Such is the importance of agenda-setting that the post-modern party increasingly regards each day as a battle to be won or lost. This expansion of traditional media management into otherwise routine or workaday events gives to post-modern communications the air of a permanent campaign.

Campaign costs
The previous two factors also help explain the burgeoning costs of post-modern communications. The urgency of finding additional funding has persuaded some parties to seek support from non-traditional sources, something which has caused controversy both within and without.

Qualitative opinion research
Traditional quantitative opinion polling is now supplemented with qualitative research. The latter is a further sign of the parties' determination to devise messages which target the most electorally significant voting groups.

Media fragmentation and narrow-casting
Campaign messages are communicated through a far wider range of media, particularly the great digital technologies: text messages, emails and web sites. More importantly, recent evidence from the USA suggests that, if they wish to fully exploit it, political parties will have to accept that digital technology will deepen the trends towards decentralised campaigning in ways that their leaderships will find difficult to control.

differentiated nature of political messages as being especially significant. If one accepts this view, the great challenge for political parties is to adapt to this very different mindset; to stop 'pushing' and more subtly 'pull' voters towards the campaign messages they offer. Whilst this thesis has yet to establish universal academic support, nonetheless it offers important new insight into the evolution of political communication. This is especially so in the aftermath of the 2008 US Presidential elections, which with good reason have been called the first elections of the digital age. The extent to which their UK counterparts are also reorientating their communications around the concept of post-modernism is likely to be one of the more interesting features of British politics over the next few years.

Conclusion

This chapter has set out some of the main trends in the history of post-war political communication. It has not attempted to provide a comprehensive, leave alone a definitive, account. Such an undertaking would be worthy of a volume in its own right. What is has tried to do, however, is demonstrate that party political communication is an increasingly complex and multi-faceted phenomenon which is rightly a subject of academic interest. What academics and others have made of it will be the overarching theme of the next four chapters.

. . . .

What you should have learnt from reading this chapter

- How to identify the broad historical phases in the evolution of party political communications, together with their distinctive features.

- An understanding of the wider electoral, political and technological contexts in which change has occurred.

- Why the evolution from pre-modern to modern can be described as uneven.

- An appreciation of the concept of post-modern communication and implications for the remainder of this study.

Glossary of key terms

Tony Benn A former Cabinet minister who became *de facto* leader of the Labour Left in the 1970s. Benn's power stemmed from his position of Chairman of the home affairs sub-committee of Labour's National Executive Committee until 1982.
Critical theorists A highly varied group of scholars and writers who have profoundly influenced the understanding of philosophy, sociology, politics and a host of other academic disciplines in the years since 1945.
Dealignment The term used to describe the breakdown in established patterns of voting beginning in the 1960s.
Philip Gould Trained in marketing, Gould joined Labour's pay roll in 1985 after being asked by Peter Mandelson to conduct some opinion research for his Shadow Communications Agency. He then worked for Labour over the next seven years before being sidelined when the party leadership passed to John Smith in 1992. However, the election of Tony Blair two years later saw Gould's return as the new leader's private pollster, a post

he retained after Labour entered office. He was subsequently ennobled as Baron Gould of Brockwood in June 2004.

Harold Macmillan Later, the Earl of Stockdale. Nicknamed 'Supermac', Macmillan led the Conservative party as prime minister from 1957 to 1963.

Lord (John) Reith The first director-general of the BBC and one of the most influential figures in the history of British broadcasting.

Suez crisis The politically disastrous attempt in 1956 by the British, French and Israeli governments to destroy the Egyptian leader, Gamal Abdul Nasser.

Tronah Mines The case of *R. v. Tronah Mines* led to a landmark ruling, as a result of which national parties were able to finance their own campaigning without breaching the strict rules governing election expenses at constituency level.

Zeitgeist The defining spirit or mood of a particular era.

 ## Likely examination questions

Distinguish between the pre-modern, modern and post-modern eras of political communication.

In what ways might we say that the emergence of modern political communication was uneven? What factors might explain this?

Why is dealignment associated with the collapse of pre-modern communication?

What explains the domination of political television?

 ## Helpful websites

The Electoral Commission, with a wealth of information on the conduct of election campaigns, can be found at www.electoralcommission.org.uk.

Suggestions for further reading

David Butler's *British General Elections since 1945* (Oxford: Blackwell, 1995) offers a useful short introduction. Dennis Kavanagh's *Election Campaigning* (Oxford: Blackwell, 1995) covers the same terrain in much more detail. An excellent conceptual analysis of the three historical phases can be found in Pippa Norris, 'Political Communication', in Patrick Dunleavy et al. (eds), *Developments in British Politics 5* (Basingstoke: Macmillan Press, 1997). Those wishing to explore the evolution of political communication within the Conservative party should consult Richard Crockett, 'The party, publicity and the media', in A. Seldon and S. Ball (eds), *The Conservative Century* (Oxford: Oxford University Press, 1994).

More recently, the history of Labour party communications has received fine treatment in Dominic Wring's *The Marketing of Labour* (Basingstoke: Palgrave Macmillan, 2005). David Denver's popular *Elections and Voting Behaviour in Britain* (2007) offers invaluable treatment of the relationship between dealignment and political communication, a work which is complemented by Nicholas Allen's 'A Restless Electorate: Stirrings in the Political Season', in J. Bartle and A. King (eds), *Britain at the Polls* (Washington, DC: CQ Press, 2006).

The Modern Communication Strategy

Contents

Overview

Chapter 2 is the first of four chapters examining particular aspects of party political communications. Here, we focus largely on the preparations parties undergo prior to major election campaigns. This entails an exploration of the communications strategy, the role of opinion research and political marketing, and the nature of campaign management. The chapter concludes by examining why some analysts believe that the highly centralised communications strategies of the modern era are becoming increasingly counter-productive.

Key issues to be covered in this chapter

- The principal features of communications strategies, illustrated by a case study of Labour's 1997 general election campaign
- The significance of political marketing and its implications for the role of political parties in representative democracies
- The War Book and communications grid as management tools
- The extent to which centralised campaign management is viable in the post-modern era

Box 2.1 Devising the strategic 'brief'

- On whose support can we rely?
- Who else do we need to vote for us?
- Of this group, who might vote for us and why?
- Where do these people typically live and how can we best reach them?
- What are our rivals likely to say about us and how might we counter them?

The communications strategy

The reality can be stated simply: 'no major British party would now dream of entering an election campaign without a communications strategy' (Kavanagh 1995: 148). What, though, is a communications strategy and why is it considered so important?

'The greatest election campaign ever'

Simply stated, a communications strategy denotes how parties organise and mobilise their communication resources in support of their wider political goals. The first task of the strategist is to devise the campaign 'messages' on which the rest of the strategy will be based. This can prove a painful experience, not least because communication strategists often insist on radical changes to organisation and policy, which many party members find difficult to accept.

Labour's ground-breaking approach in 1997 sheds some light on the process parties undergo as they devise their key campaign messages. Prior to the election, the Blair leadership was clear about one thing: Labour's image 'as a party of the poor and of the past' doomed it to perpetual electoral failure (Gould 1998: 176). Despite public opinion poll evidence that voters were disavowing Thatcherism, Labour's private research suggested strongly that the Conservative vision of an ideal society still corresponded more to the Britain most voters wanted for themselves and their families. For all their dissatisfaction with the Tories, therefore, most voters did not believe that the Labour party understood the nature of their hopes for a better tomorrow. A series

Box 2.2 The issues shaping Labour's 1997 communication strategy

Labour's weaknesses
A poor reputation in respect of tax, interest rates and inflation; fears of the latent power of the Labour Left; and '**Middle England**'s' innate mistrust of change.

Conservative strengths
An improving economy; patriotism; and a widespread view that, for all their faults, the Conservatives were a known quantity.

Conservative weaknesses
The party had been in office for too long; they were only interested in the needs of the (wealthy) few; they could not be trusted; they were hampered by weak leadership; they had a poor record in managing the key public services.

Labour's strengths
Tony Blair was widely seen as a prime minister-in-waiting; Blair conveyed the prospect of a better future and the desirability of change, whilst Labour was perceived as having a historic capacity to represent the needs of the many.

(*Source:* Gould 1998)

of highly public initiatives – notably the rewriting of **Clause IV** of the party's 1918 constitution – had been used to convey the impression that the Labour party was ready to change and move on. Yet neither Blair nor his advisers were under any illusion that these would be of lasting electoral value. Too many voters still distrusted Labour. The Conservatives knew this and would counter-attack accordingly.

Thanks in part to the extensive use of private opinion research, Labour's strategists identified the themes they believed would dominate the forthcoming campaign. These were then used to construct the five core messages that they hoped would neutralise the party's weaknesses and promote its strengths:

- Leadership
- A party for the many, not the few

- The future
- Enough is enough (a comment on John Major's premiership)
- Britain deserves better

These messages were reinforced by the decision to make a limited number of very specific policy pledges. This re-emphasised the theme of *real* leadership: Labour would not commit itself in opposition to any promise it could not fulfil in office.

The subsequent development of Labour's propaganda, including its political advertising, was dominated by the need to ensure that these five messages appeared consistently and repetitively. Labour did this so well that the clarity and directness of its campaigning disorientated the Conservatives. In their confusion, they devised three counter-strategies, before finally adopting 'New Labour, New Danger' in April 1996. However, despite attracting much media comment, especially when the notorious 'demon eyes' poster was released two months later, Labour believed this to be the least effective option.

- Firstly, it confirmed their claim that Blair's party was new.
- Secondly, nothing in its opinion research suggested that voters believed a new incarnation of the Labour party posed any danger at all: it was 'old' Labour that worried them.
- Thirdly, it threw out the timing of the Conservatives' own campaigning. Instead of admitting to voters that mistakes had been made (especially in respect of fiscal policy and the public services) before pointing to the recent upturn in the main economic indicators, the Conservatives went on to the offensive too early.
- Finally, it gave their campaign a very negative tone and helped Labour's own campaigners convince voters that, after 18 years, the Tories had nothing new to offer.

As the Conservative counter-attack floundered, it is unsurprising that a self-congratulatory mood developed among the staff at **Millbank**: hence the title of this sub-section. It is, of course, arguable that Labour would have won the 1997 general election regardless of other factors. Whether it would have done so with a 179-seat majority, thereby effectively guaranteeing a second term in office, is less certain.

Box 2.3 The long campaign in 2004–5

The three main parties all showcased commitments designed to appeal to their target voters. **Labour** promised help to first-time buyers and promoted new employment rights for pregnant women. The **Conservatives** highlighted failings within the NHS and offered extended relief on council tax for the elderly. In addition, Michael Howard promised measures to control a number of unpopular minorities: ill-disciplined school children, travellers and illegal immigrants. The **Liberal Democrats'** commitments overlapped those of the other two parties. Charles Kennedy pledged to increase both maternity pay and pensions for the very old.

The long campaign

Parties also prefer to test their messages via the long campaign. This is associated with Ronald Reagan's 1984 bid to retain the US Presidency and was imported into the UK by the Conservative party eight years later. However, in addition to the all-important testing, the long campaign also enables the parties to seize the news agenda some months before polling. This, indeed, was the primary objective of Reagan's campaign team, which used the long campaign to focus attention on the unpopularity of Democrat policy on law and order and defence and away from the economic recession that threatened to reverse Republican gains among blue-collar workers. This aspect of the long campaign has become all the more important as rival strategists have shown a remarkable ability to anticipate each other's main lines of attack and counter-attack. Consequently, they now vie to set the campaign agenda some months before polling, both by impressing media commentators and forcing their opponents onto the defensive (Butler and Kavanagh 2006: 53). Theory and reality, however, do not always coincide. This was especially so in 2005. Despite Labour's long campaign being nearly derailed by the so-called '**battle of the books**', it was too far ahead for these internal problems to undermine its lead.

Communication strategies in the age of devolution

Devolution has also influenced communication strategies in both Wales and Scotland, where it is now clear that the principal nationalist parties focus their resources on their respective regional contests. This is especially so in Scotland, where SNP spending in 2007 fell just short of the permitted maximum of £1,516,000. In the process, Alex Salmond and his colleagues spent £280,000 more than Labour, £780,000 more than the Conservatives and a massive £1,080,000 more than the Liberal Democrats. The SNP's strategy was hugely successful. Its likely impact on a cash-strapped Scottish Labour Party, which will be almost certainly compelled to fight the next Scottish Parliament elections one year after a general election it seems destined to lose, can be all too easily guessed at.

Table 2.1 Central campaign expenditure of the nationalist parties of Scotland and Wales (selected items)

Item	Scottish National Party (£s)		Plaid Cymru (£s)	
	2007 Scottish Parliament election	2005 general election	2007 Welsh Assembly election	2005 general election
Party political broadcasts	90,726	41,607	22,500	2,233
Advertisements	494,642	40,111	78,814	15,105
Mail shots, etc.	323,580	30,165	86,714	1,882
Market research	178,705	26,090	38,063	14,613
Media	45,041	28,398	5,420	0
Total	**1,383,462**	**193,987**	**261,286**	**38,879**

(*Source:* Electoral Commission)

Tails wagging dogs: opinion research and the rise of political marketing

New Labour's communications strategy in 1997 is not merely of historic interest. More than any other campaign, it illuminates the enduring controversy over the proper use of private opinion research, which has been for some years 'a key influence on the content, style and means of delivery of party propaganda' (Rosenbaum 1997: 147).

Box 2.4 Categories of opinion research

Quantitative polling
This measures voter responses over a period of time and can be divided into two main sub-groups. *Tracking surveys* ask the same question to different people at different times and are especially useful in monitoring or 'tracking' changes in public opinion. Elsewhere, *panel studies* concentrate on the same sample of voters to gain more detailed insight into changing voter attitudes.

Qualitative polling
By contrast, qualitative polling explains *why* certain groups of voters think in the way they do. The most popular method is the *focus group*: a small group of volunteers chosen because of their individual profiles. A variant of the focus group is *people-metering* or *'pulsing'*. This was introduced in the UK in 1989 by the celebrated US pollster Richard Wirthlin and requires volunteers to respond to clips on a TV screen by pressing buttons on electronic handsets. The instantaneous responses enable pollsters to 'identify exactly which visual, verbal or thematic components score and which are counterproductive (Rosenbaum 1997: 173). It also allows the pollsters to follow up with focus group-style discussions, though Rosenbaum (1997: 174) questions the extent to which it has revolutionised opinion research in the years which followed.

Psychographics
Wirthlin is also associated with a technique known as 'psychographics'. This works by attempting to place various categories of voter into 'value-groups', the belief being that party choice is ultimately determined by these latent values. This technique was briefly adopted by the Conservative party from 1986, only to be dropped by Party Chairman Chris Patten on the grounds of cost-effectiveness.

Parties commission private opinion polls for two broad purposes. One of these is campaign polling. Despite being used extensively by the two main parties (Rosenbaum 1997: 165), it is questionable whether it is of any real value. Secondly, and as implied above, its other use is to design the communications strategy. For marketing experts (Lees-Marshment 2001), this is an inevitable consequence of the attitudinal trends and collapse of ideological difference discussed in the previous chapter. Others are less convinced and argue that the extended use of opinion research simply reveals the extent to which some parties have abandoned altogether the '**educationalist mission**' which remains a critical part of their role in a healthy democratic polity.

Opinion research and political marketing

This controversy has attracted considerable academic attention. At the heart of the debate lies the distinction between two rival concepts: 'political sales' and 'political marketing'. Those parties engaged in political marketing base their political communication on the completion of four very distinctive tasks (Lees-Marshment 2001: 23):

- Ensuring that their 'product' (policies, manifesto, leadership) is designed to maximise voter appeal
- Evaluating all those factors which are likely to influence this
- Devising a strategy to compete effectively with rival businesses
- Integrating all aspects of the party around the single goal of enhanced sales (that is, increased votes)

Put simply, parties basing their communications on marketing never attempt to *create* demand for their product. Instead, they use opinion research to ascertain precisely what it is voters want and design their product accordingly. It follows that voters will always 'buy' what is on offer, since the latter will have been carefully structured around their stated preferences. This can be seen in Box 2.6.

For the market-orientated party, opinion research (market intelligence) precedes all other stages. Whereas the sales-orientated party uses market intelligence to identify the best ways of selling a product which has been designed already, its market-orientated rival uses its intelligence both to design its product and, later, to adjust it to ensure maximum market penetration. Lees-Marshment (2001: 37) strongly

Box 2.5 Private opinion research and the 2005 general election

The Labour party

As was the case in both 1997 and 2001, Labour used opinion research far more extensively than its two main rivals (Butler and Kavanagh 2006: 89). Labour's polling had three main elements:

- The party's chief pollster, Mark Penn, conducted a monthly tracking poll from September 2004, complemented by a separate weekly tracking poll conducted by YouGov.
- Between November 2004 and March 2005 his predecessor, Stan Greenberg, carried out quantitative research in 130 target marginals, supplemented by a multi-faceted focus group operation.
- Labour also continued its polling during the campaign. A 2,100 sample poll was revisited every 4–5 days from April onwards, with at least 15 focus groups being conducted at the same time. Three late changes to Labour's campaign – Blair's engagement with voters via audience-participation TV and radio programmes; populist initiatives on immigration and antisocial behaviour; and the U-turn over the decision to marginalise Gordon Brown – can all be traced to the influence of this research.

The Conservative party

The Conservatives' efforts were hampered by the decision of ICM to sever its connections with the party after seven months, the contract being awarded to ORB (Opinion Research Business) in June 2004.

- ORB conducted tracking polls in 163 target constituencies focusing on those voters who had backed Labour in 2001 but had since become undecided.
- During the campaign it contacted 500 of these voters per night, the results of which were collated every three days for consideration by Michael Howard and his team.
- Qualitative research through 90 focus groups was also conducted in the target constituencies between June 2004 and polling day.

The Liberal Democrat party

The Liberal Democrats' polling took more or less the same form as it did in both 1997 and 2001: a tracking poll of target voters in the 40 seats the party was most determined to win.

Box 2.6 The communication strategies of the product-, sales- and market-orientated parties

Product-orientated parties	Sales-orientated parties	Market-orientated parties
Product design	Product design	Market intelligence
Communication	Market intelligence	Product design
Campaign	Communication	Product adjustment
Election	Campaign	Implementation
Delivery	Election	Communication
	Delivery	Campaign
		Election
		Delivery

(*Source:* Lees-Marshment 2001)

emphasises that the twin processes of design and adjustment will inevitably produce something that is most unlikely to meet the needs of traditional supporters. Hence the need for an additional 'implementation' phase, when the leadership aims to convince the rest of the party to endorse a product which may challenge some of its most deeply held beliefs.

The extent to which the UK's main parties consistently fit the market-orientated typology is disputed, though it is worth noting that Lees-Marshment herself was highly critical of what she saw as an ill-conceived and half-hearted commitment to marketing in the 2005 general election (Lees-Marshment and Roberts 2005). Equally, it is undeniable that political marketing has played a key role in the debate over Tony Blair's leadership of the Labour party. New Labour's extensive use of opinion research during this time is a matter of record (Lees-Marshment 2001: 184). This has exposed it to two criticisms:

• Firstly, that it deliberately manufactured opinion research data in its internal battles with party traditionalists. This is the view of Dominic Wring (2005: 122, 130), who argues that the uncritical collation of the views of focus groups chosen precisely because they had rejected Labour was bound to produce evidence endorsing the Blairites' clamour for change.

- Secondly, and more importantly, New Labour has had to face down persistent criticisms that the wholesale changes to party policy that followed were made solely with reference to the views (and prejudices) of its focus groups and the newspapers they tended to read. Inevitably, such accusations were fuelled by unattributed comments from Blair's team to the effect that '[i]n the mass media age, policy is there to win elections' (quoted in Butler and Kavanagh 1997: 61). Particularly galling to New Labour's internal critics was the ceding of whole swathes of political territory – on taxation and spending, public ownership and regulation, civil liberties and immigration – to neo-conservatives, even when the latter's position on these and a host of other issues was very much open to challenge (Wring 2005: 161–79).

Sadly, this is not the proper place for an evaluation of these criticisms, though it is only fair to note that other observers dispute that Blairism should be dismissed simply as a marketing gimmick (Faucher-King 2009). More generally, it might be argued that even the most enthusiastic devotees of political marketing cannot detach themselves completely from their parties' histories or ideological traditions. Parties have collective images, which give rise to popular and enduring assumptions about what the electorate can expect of them. Ignoring them courts disaster: party leaders and MPs would divide against each other; the core vote would be alienated; and floating voters would be left confused (Wring 2005: 2–4).

Centralised campaign management

The controversy over political marketing shows that the seemingly humble communications strategy has the power to provoke comment and debate, a point which also extends to the 'all-pervasive' central campaign management (Butler and Kavanagh 1992: 77). Despite the association of campaign management with excessive levels of internal discipline, much more is involved than merely keeping people 'on message'. Rather, the principal task of campaign managers is to ensure that their strategy and core messages are condensed and reproduced in a format that will survive contact with the enemy. This is a huge organisational and logistical task, made all the more demanding by the fact that national party organisations have increasingly taken responsibility for constituency campaigning in the target seats.

The 'War Book' and 'communications grid'

To assist in forming a communications strategy, campaign managers have devised two important management tools. The first of these is known as the War Book, which has been described as:

> . . . a bulky file . . . containing daily programmes for press conferences, photo-opportunities, rallies, broadcasts, schedules of main speakers, advertisements, posters and other events. Each War Book also contains material on the party's strengths and weaknesses, suggestions for deflecting the attacks of the opposition, and proposals for promoting favoured issues and themes. It [also] includes advice on how to cope with known future events. (Butler and Kavanagh 1992: 77)

The benefits of the War Book are strongly emphasised by veteran US Democrat strategist Joe Napolitan, who maintains that a communication strategy must be written up in this way or else it will simply unravel in the heat of battle.

A second management tool – the communications grid – works to the same effect. This is described by Philip Gould (1998: 335–6) as 'the heart of an election campaign . . . the point at which strategy, message and logistics all gel on one single piece of paper'. The grid sets out the timetable detailing the main events on each day's campaigning. In addition, it will identify and settle a variety of logistical concerns. Typically, these will include:

- identifying the main campaigners;
- selecting appropriate venues and audiences for the 'campaign trail';
- dealing with the array of transport, accommodation and security issues involved;
- ensuring that the media are on hand to report these events;
- providing effective photo opportunities and sound bites for television news crews and ensuring these are delivered in time for the main lunchtime and evening TV news bulletins;
- reconciling the grid with the targeting strategy;

- coordinating the activities of those on the campaign trail with those working in campaign headquarters;
- acquiring a strategic capacity to modify each day's campaigning as events dictate; and finally
- creating an internal communication infrastructure to ensure that all candidates are kept fully aware of campaign developments.

The grid will also identify a dominant theme for each day's campaigning. This will be revealed at the daily morning press conference and reinforced by those politicians on the campaign trail at events throughout the day. The selected theme will be also taken up by the press and publicity officers as they consider the most appropriate sound bite and televisual photo opportunities. The net effect is that the communications grid will be overlaid with a separate 'message grid' to which all the leading campaigners will be expected to adhere.

Drafting these documents can be a lengthy process. Prior to the 1997 general election, Labour's draft War Book passed through five focus groups – **swing voters** (switchers from Conservative to Labour), women, first-time voters, the DE voters (Labour's historic core; essentially this refers to unskilled workers, the unemployed and those solely dependent upon state benefits), and constituencies across the Pennine Belt (Labour's target marginals) – before being handed to the party leadership for approval. Further work was then done by Paul Begala, a senior consultant to Bill Clinton. According to Gould (1998: 336–7), Mandelson's draft communications and message grid was subsequently 'discussed at countless meetings and went through a dozen redrafts' between January and April 1997 before being presented to Blair and Brown.

Flexibility and responsiveness
However, the hidden secret of effective central campaign management is the ability to prevent strict adherence to the War Book from degenerating into a dysfunctional rigidity. Consequently, a key feature of campaign management is round-the-clock monitoring and daily reassessments: the daily schedule only being finalised one day in advance. The dominant theme is rebuttal: to anticipate opposition (and media) attacks and have responses prepared. Similarly, where

the data reveals that the opposition is on the defensive, the next day's campaigning can be modified to exploit this.

The business of review and reflection continues throughout the rest of the day – and night. In 2005, for example, designated campaign staff worked into the small hours collating information sent to them by national and local canvassers, along with their own assessments of the first editions of the morning's newspapers. Their findings were then forwarded to party strategists who would meet prior to the morning press conference to agree the final content of the day's campaigning. This technique was central to the Democrats' successful 1992 Presidential campaign and has since been used consistently in the UK.

Targeting

This is the most important recent development in campaign management, a point I shall take up in more detail in the following chapter. For some experts 'the campaigns in the [target] constituencies now dominate the parties' overall campaign strategy' (Fisher et al. 2005: 18). This has presented campaign managers with a completely new set of managerial and logistical problems, which extend from determining the extent of the targeting, through the coordination of canvassing and 'knocking up' operations, to overseeing direct mailing and the many other forms of direct marketing. In addition, parties now prefer to use information technology to assist in this, something which means that responsibility for the increasingly large voter databases and data management software has also fallen to national managers. Fisher and his colleagues note that parties committed to targeting now have bespoke sections within their organisations devoted to this task and channel most of their campaign resources and efforts through them (2005).

Process journalism, campaign discipline and digital communications

Given the above, it is hardly surprising that national campaign managers insist on such a high degree of discipline. It is axiomatic that the more complex the operation, the more prone it is to internal breakdown. However, the media also bears some responsibility for this. Rightly or wrongly, media reporting of elections is dominated by the electoral 'process'. Not only do national campaigners have to work much harder to ensure that their messages receive media coverage, but also their efforts can be completely undermined whenever a candidate's comments merely hint at internal disagreement or confusion. The Conservative party, for example, found to its cost in both 2001 and 2005 how easily its communication strategy could be derailed, when both Oliver Letwin and later Howard Flight made injudicious comments at critical points during the campaign.

The notoriety of central campaign management has grown significantly with the ever wider use of digital technology. Whilst the value of the email and text messaging in communicating with voters is open to question, they have become indispensible tools in ensuring that the daily adjustments to the communications grid are efficiently communicated to candidates. In 1997, the parties were making contact with their candidates two to three times per day, a trend which was strengthened in both 2001 and 2005.

> Although the internet may not have reached – let alone influenced – many voters, the parties' private intranets were enormously important in enabling daily or twice daily instant messages to every candidate. . . . As one Labour insider said: 'We don't reach the mass public through the internet but it does allow us to promote the three Ms: to spread our Message to our own people, to Mobilise them and to get Money out of them. (Butler and Kavanagh 2006: 173)

Some candidates undoubtedly welcome these developments, not least because they are forewarned about likely media questions and how to answer them. At the same time, Ballinger (2002: 219–20) notes that others are increasingly resentful of what they see as the extreme negativity of the central directives. In this way we arrive at the great paradox of centralised campaign management. Whilst it enables party political communication to acquire an internal coherence utterly absent in the pre-modern era, this has come with a price tag far exceeding the financial cost of equipping a national campaign headquarters. This factor, along with its implications for future communications strategies, is the subject of the next section.

From Millbank to Old Queen Street

The debate over the long-term viability of the top-down strategies of the 1990s was captured in the decision of leading party officials to disband Labour's famous campaign headquarters at Millbank in August 2002. Campaign management was instead relocated to smaller and less obtrusive premises in Old Queen Street. For all its strengths, the Millbank model was prone to at least four weaknesses:

- Firstly, it proved highly vulnerable to internal division at the top of the party hierarchy. This was very visible prior to the 2005 general election. The Labour party's campaign was very nearly derailed by Blair's decision to replace Gordon Brown as campaign and policy coordinator with Alan Milburn, one of Brown's bitterest critics, on 12 September 2004. This subsequently led to a series of damaging tit-for-tat media exchanges, which only ended after Blair bowed before adverse opinion research and brought back Brown into the campaign.
- Secondly, there is a strong sense that the Millbank model became self-defeating. Labour's success in communicating its campaign messages both encouraged its rivals to follow suit and the media to join the fray through a technique known as strategic framing. This assumes that party communications are always heavily 'spun' and, further, that journalists have a duty to decode and explain this to the electorate. This has only exacerbated the general tendency towards **process journalism**. Worse, the electorate was deluged with information on a scale which made it even harder for the parties to communicate their key campaign messages.
- Thirdly, as mentioned above, the top-down nature of this type of campaigning risked alienating individuals in the constituencies. Indeed, far from compensating for the decline of local parties, it is arguable that, by emphasising control and restraint so strongly, the Millbank approach may have actually contributed to it. Only the most committed are likely to give up their time to campaign in such circumstances, which, given the general antipathy towards party politics, will rarely amount to more than a handful of people. This will obviously impact on a party's ability to call on the support of volunteers and leaves it still further exposed to accusations of 'control freakery'.
- Finally, a question remains as to whether this approach actually justifies the human and financial resources devoted to it. The campaign management discussed above exists solely to 'push' a party's

messages to the electorate. Yet there is growing evidence that the latter are no longer prepared to accept this. Too often they either feel that they are being 'talked at' or that an elaborate attempt is being made to deceive them – 'spin' replacing 'sleaze' as the common descriptor of the machinations of a cynical, self-serving political elite.

Antipathy to political parties is felt particularly strongly among first-time voters. In the 2001 general election, the overall turnout of 59.38 per cent was disappointing enough. However, among first-time voters this figure dropped to a desperate 21 per cent. Research commissioned by the Economic and Research Council subsequently found that younger people invariably dismissed the parties' campaign messages as patronising, confusing and dull (Coughlan 2001). The fact that this younger generation of 'digital natives' increasingly rejects the mass media as its principal source of political information weakened still further the impact of the national campaign. If true, it follows that parties will have to develop new types of communications strategy which effectively seek the 'permission' of the audience before engaging with them (Butler and Kavanagh 2006: 18). Given the hierarchical nature of most political parties, this could prove their most daunting if interesting challenge yet.

Conclusion

There is very little evidence that the major parties significantly modified their communication strategies prior to the 2005 general election. However, in the years that have followed, developments in the USA in particular suggest that it is only a matter of time before they will feel compelled to do so. This could have major consequences not simply for communication strategies, but also for the parties themselves. Above all, it implies that they will have to abandon their current thinking on political campaigning and build a new approach based upon the culture surrounding digital technology. In short, they will have to go into what one observer refers to as 'receive mode' and accept that 'the party is no longer the be-all and end-all, but merely the centre of a movement – a network of activists' (Colville 2008: 22). To find out why, we must in the next chapter revisit two concepts that had seemed completely out of date during the Millbank era: retail politics and the constituency campaign.

· ·

 What you should have learnt from reading this chapter

• An understanding of the nature and purpose of a communication strategy.

• Why campaign managers rely on private opinion researchers and why their work is increasingly controversial.

• The reasons why an effective strategy is associated with a comprehensive War Book and communication/message grid.

• The reasons why centralised campaign management of the last two decades may be coming to an end.

 Glossary of key terms

'Battle of the books' The tit-for-tat revelations put into the public domain by the respective supporters of Blair and Brown in January 2005, as they jockeyed for supremacy within the Labour party. With a general election just months away, this episode revealed just how far the relationship between the two men had deteriorated. ˙

Clause IV Clause IV of the Labour Party's 1918 constitution famously committed it to the 'common ownership' of the economy and redistribution of wealth. For party traditionalists, therefore, it captured the essence of Labour's socialist commitment and distinguished it from its political rivals.

Educationalist mission The belief that party political communications should aim to win converts to a political cause, rather than simply garner votes.

Middle England A popular term used to denote lower-middle and middle-class voters living in English outer suburban and rural constituencies. Since 1979, gaining the support of this rather variegated group has been regarded as absolutely essential for success in British general elections.

Millbank The name of the campaign headquarters purchased by Labour in 1995 and subsequently used as a political shorthand for heavily centralised campaign management.

Process journalism (electoral process) A style of election reporting, which focuses exclusively on the changing fortunes of the main antagonists at the expense of the issues and key policies.

Swing voters Generally, this term refers to those voters who switch allegiance ('swing') from one party to another between elections. More specifically, it denotes those voting groups that have a propensity to do this and, as a result, determine the final outcome of an election.

Likely examination questions

What is a modern communication strategy and why do the major political parties believe such a strategy is now an essential feature of campaign success?

Explain the multi-dimensional role of opinion research in election campaigning. Why is this development so controversial?

Why do national party leaders insist on managing campaigns so comprehensively?

Helpful websites

The work of opinion poll companies can be accessed via the websites of leading firms such as www.ipsos-mori.com and www.gallup.com. The British Polling Council (www.britishpollingcouncil.org) has a very informative section on its website which offers a detailed guide on opinion polling, whilst www.electoral-vote.com offers a similar service albeit from a North American perspective.

Suggestions for further reading

Undoubtedly the best insider account of devising a communication strategy and managing a national campaign is Philip Gould's *The Unfinished Revolution* (1998). Martin Rosenbaum's *From Soapbox to Soundbite* provides a very informed history of the use of private opinion research, whilst Jennifer Lees-Marshment (2001) and Dominic Wring (2005) are essential reading for the debate on political marketing. Finally, it remains the case that the Nuffield series offers the most authoritative and accessible accounts of party campaigning in general elections.

CHAPTER 3

Constituency Campaigning in the Post-Modern Age

Contents

Overview

Constituency campaigning was the bedrock of party political communication for the first half of the twentieth century, after which it seemed to go into near terminal decline. More recently, however, there is evidence that it is enjoying something of a revival, albeit in a much revised form. This chapter seeks to explain these processes and, more importantly, what they mean for the relationship between national campaign managers and constituency activists. It concludes by examining how we might expect this relationship to change further still, something which leads inevitably to an analysis of Barack Obama's campaign for the US Presidency in 2008.

Key issues to be covered in this chapter

- Why constituency campaigning still matters
- The nature and methods of targeting
- The use of voter databases and management software
- The role played by digital communications in the revival of constituency campaigning
- The 2008 US Presidential election and its lessons for the UK

The limitations of the national campaign

For a century and more, the constituency campaign was the dominant means of party political communication. Aside from making the case on the doorstep, local volunteers also recorded the location of potential supporters and organised get-out-the-vote (GOTV), or 'knocking up', operations on polling day. However, whilst local campaigning remained a valuable tool for the many parties with limited financial resources, the two main parties increasingly downgraded it in favour of national advertising and mediated communications. The reasons

Table 3.1 Sources of political information over the general election campaigns 1997, 2001 and 2005 (figures as percentage of the electorate)

	1997 (voters who confirmed they...)	2001 (voters who confirmed they...	2005 (voters who confirmed they...)
Mediated communications			
Saw leaders on TV	36	43	46
Political advertising			
Saw TV PEBs	73	58	70
Saw posters	70	50	62
Saw press advertisements	not available	37	48
Heard radio PEBs	15	16	20
Retail politics			
Received leaflets	89	69	89
Were called upon	24	14	21
Received personal letter	20	12	21
Were telephoned	7	5	7
Received party video/DVD	not available	1	3
Received party email	not available	1	3

(*Source:* Butler and Kavanagh 2002: 214; Butler and Kavanagh 2006: 169)

for this have been articulated in Chapter 1. Meanwhile, buoyed by the professionalism of their national campaigning, party managers concluded that they could reach voters more effectively without the help of well-meaning but often amateurish and ill-disciplined local campaigners. Academic commentators agreed, the 'traditional' view being that, if campaigning made a difference at all, it was the national campaign alone which counted (Fisher et al. 2005: 1).

Yet from the mid 1990s onwards, a new generation of academic commentators (the 'revisionists') questioned this perspective and concluded that national parties should actually encourage campaigning at constituency level. In addition to the various criticisms of the so-called Millbank model made at the end of the previous chapter, evidence began to accrue that the broad thrust of the national campaign was being parried by vast numbers of voters (Butler and Kavanagh 1992: 231). In their joint analysis of the 2001 general election, Mori and the Electoral Commission in 2001 concurred and suggested that neither national advertisements nor party election broadcasts (PEBs) had a significant impact on voting behaviour (Butler and Kavanagh 2002: 214).

Targeting and the revival of constituency campaigning

The parties' response has been to refocus their communications on very particular groups of voters. In itself, this is nothing new. The parties have been aware long since that voters with certain social characteristics are more likely to 'swing' from one side to another and, further, that attracting the support of such people is likely to make the difference between winning and losing. The history of Conservative communications alone offers numerous instances of this. Since the 1880s the Tories have known that their electoral fortunes depend upon the support of the working rather than the middle class. In the years which followed, they refined this understanding to a point where they successfully identified specific sub-groups who might prove particularly susceptible to their campaign messages. In 1970, for example, they targeted the wives of working-class Labour voters. Nine years later they turned towards the so-called **'new' working class**. This was the age of 'Basildon Man', whose willingness to abandon Labour for the Conservatives powered the latter to four successive general election victories after 1979.

Beginning in 1992, however, the character of targeting began to change quite noticeably. Primarily, it acquired a heightened geographical dimension (Fisher et al. 2005: 2). Each party now identifies a relatively small number of '**battleground constituencies**' (inevitably they tend to identify the same ones) at whom the overwhelming majority of their campaigning is directed (Fisher et al. 2005: 18). An important corollary of this is that those voters living elsewhere are effectively ignored. The resulting bifurcation is noted by the authors of the 2005 Nuffield Study 'Constituency campaigning is changing rapidly, decaying in most places yet becoming more sophisticated . . . in marginal seats' (Butler and Kavanagh: 2006: 176). This approach, which is not easily reconciled with the ethos of democracy, nonetheless can be justified with reference to the 'iron law' of plural voting. One unnamed Conservative captured this with disturbing precision when he pointed out that, of the 7.4 million voters in his party's main target seats, only 838,000 – those whose shifting loyalty from Labour to the Conservatives would have been enough to return a Conservative government – really mattered (Butler and Kavanagh 2006: 170). The spatially focused nature of targeting is apparent in Box 3.1.

The second great change concerned the way in which information technology was used to identify the precise location *within each constituency* of the voters whose social characteristics and known or estimated attitudes were most likely to affect the outcome. In the past, the task of gathering such data would have fallen on local volunteers and, whilst it remains the case that some local parties still attempt to do this, such efforts are not particularly rewarding. As a result, national managers now look to a range of alternative intelligence-gathering and -processing techniques to help them identify the locations of their key voters.

- The starting point of this exercise is the electoral register, a copy of which is distributed to all constituency parties by local authority returning officers.
- Locally generated intelligence, including canvassing returns from the previous election, can be added to this as a second layer.

Box 3.1 Targeting in the 2005 general election

Labour's targeting was purely defensive: it poured its resources into 107 seats which it believed it could hold, though most were spent on an 'inner core' of 45.

The **Liberal Democrat** strategy was more positive but equally straightforward. Lacking the resources and the prospect of outright victory, it focused on what it saw as a realistic number of gains: some 20 to 30 seats. As a result, the Liberal Democrats left their sitting MPs to themselves.

The **Conservatives**, in this as in so much else, found themselves with a dilemma. Led by the Co-Chairman, Lord Saatchi, key figures in the party argued that the Tories should target all 163 seats needed for a slim majority. This approach was bitterly opposed by others, including Lord Ashcroft, who made £2 million available to 41 constituency associations fighting the most marginal seats. A further 39 received similar support from Lord Steinberg and the Midlands Industrial Council.

Increasingly, however, the two main parties now choose to supplement this with telephone canvassing organised by their respective national party machines.

- However, following US trends a third layer is now added to the data-gathering process: commercial databases. These are generated by various companies working for large-scale corporations, a particularly well known example of which is Experian's MOSAIC.

MOSAIC divides the adult population into 61 separate categories, which are then used to evaluate their tastes and consumer behaviour. However, and in addition, parties believe that the social characteristics of such a stratified range of groups can be used also to identify likely voting behaviour. In this way, commercial databases plug any number of gaps in a party's internally generated intelligence. That MOSAIC cross-references this information against postcode areas helps parties still further to identify where their target voters are most likely to live.

Voters should be wary of underestimating the parties' ability to accumulate vast amounts of personal data (Gardner 2006). This is especially so in the US where both the Republicans and Democrats have each accumulated databases on over 160 million individuals.

Data management software: the case of Voter Vault

The key to successful targeting, however, is less how data is gathered than how it is managed. At the 2005 general election, the Conservative party demonstrated this by using management software to refine their knowledge of how individuals appearing on their databases, or living in the key postal areas, were likely to vote. They did this by purchasing from the US Republican party the Voter Vault system. Based on MOSAIC and built by the Seattle-based Advanced Custom Software, Voter Vault had been successfully used by the Republicans in the Congressional elections of 2002 and 2006, together with the Presidential elections of 2004. According to Liam Fox, then Co-Chairman of the party, Voter Vault helped the Republican party to increase its vote by 4 per cent in 2006. On paper, this is a seemingly small amount. However, it was still enough to help it strengthen its hold on both houses of Congress.

Inevitably, this attracted the interest of Conservative campaign managers, who used it to locate voters with the following characteristics: a high propensity to vote; a basic affinity with the Conservative party; and a refusal to vote Conservative in 2001. Voter Vault does this by setting the known social characteristics of an individual against the known social characteristics of those who are already known to be committed to a particular party. (The Conservatives used the characteristics of 20,000 of their own members to create this comparator.) With the latter serving as a template, the software then 'vaults' the data held on the individual to predict how he or she is likely to vote. According to internal Conservative sources, the reliability of Voter Vault is highly impressive. In one trial using a sample of 340,000 voters, the Conservatives found that they could predict with an accuracy of 82 per cent who would vote for them (Watt and Borger 2004).

This type of data management brings unprecedented efficiency to both canvassing and GOTV operations. Only those people identified as having a high likelihood of voting for a particular party will be spoken to by canvassers. Their responses can be recorded on the database and arrangements can be put in place to ensure that they are contacted again (and again) before polling day.

Making the case: direct marketing in the digital age

Though targeting is undoubtedly linked to the revival of constituency campaigning, it is clearly some distance removed from the traditional image of local volunteers tramping up and down streets in a valiant effort to get out the party vote. Indeed, Labour's general secretary in 2005 acknowledged as much when he observed that 'if local campaigning were to work [sic], local party workers increasingly had to be helped by professionals employed at the centre' (Butler and Kavanagh: 2006: 19). This is confirmed by Fisher and his colleagues, who note that 'National party professionals . . . seek to exercise much greater control over local campaigning by managing key constituency campaigns . . . and integrating them much more closely into the national effort (Fisher et al. 2005: 3).

In addition, central control is further enhanced by the means by which campaign messages are actually communicated at local level. Of the traditional techniques, one – the public meeting – has effectively disappeared, whilst a further two – poster campaigns and door-step canvassing – are seemingly in terminal decline. Three others – the electoral address delivered free by the Royal Mail, leafleting delivered by party activists, and knocking-up operations – are still used but without any evidence to suggest that they are particularly effective.

The result is akin to a partial vacuum which the distinctly modern techniques of direct marketing have sought to fill. More importantly, given their resource and logistical implications, these are provided either directly or indirectly by central party organisations. Data management software simply reinforces this process. Once the appropriate data has been processed, national campaign managers can use it to personalise political communication to an unprecedented degree. This is clear from the last general election. In addition to providing the bulk of direct mailing, national parties were responsible for 46 per cent of constituency leaflets and an increasing share of telephone canvassing (Fisher et al. 2005).

Direct mail and telephone canvassing

Direct mailing has a well-established tradition, dating from the 1920s. According to Rosenbaum (1997: 215) it was apparent by the late 1960s that computer technology would open a new era in direct mail since 'it allowed for individual letters to be fully personalised and the text to be varied according to the occupation of the recipients'. However, it was not until the 1987 general election that the parties finally began to take full advantage of this. Thereafter, thanks to the voter databases and software such as Labour's Contact Creator and Print Creator, the personalisation of direct mail and the volume of mail shots have continued to grow. In the 2005 general election, over one-in-five voters acknowledged receipt of a personal letter, with Labour alone admitting to sending out over ten million items of direct mail from its centre in Gosforth (Butler and Kavanagh 2006: 177). The same technology has also helped the central party organisations to influence the content of local leaflets.

The other strategic form of direct marketing available to national campaign managers is the centralised telephone canvass. Since 1997, the Labour party has used this technique to obtain vital information on the voting intentions of voters in its target constituencies. A huge amount of this work is done by the designated call centre expressly established for this purpose. By 2005, it was estimated that the 120 staff employed there made over two million calls during the campaign. Their efforts will be supplemented by those of local party volunteers who will also be allocated calls and it should be noted that, as the average age of party members continues to rise, this is something which is proving more popular with older party members.

The internet and digital communications

The other key development in the area of direct marketing is the use of digital technology. All the UK parties have their own websites, with 66 per cent of constituency parties going online at local level. In addition, there have been various experiments with other forms of digital communications such as creating pages on the most popular social networking sites and sending emails and text messages.

Aside from the benefits to organisational efficiency discussed in Chapter 2, the digital revolution offers numerous advantages to professional communicators.

- Firstly, it puts them firmly in charge of the communications process. The case of the Democratic Unionist Party (DUP) offers an interesting if somewhat unsuspected case in point. Despite its ultra-traditional image, the DUP became one of the first UK parties to embrace digital communications with real enthusiasm. The key reason for this unlikely development lay in the party's long-standing hostility towards the media, which it continually accused of distorting its messages.
- Secondly, when compared to political advertising, it is a highly cost-effective ways of campaigning.
- Thirdly, and perhaps most importantly, digital technology enables parties to customise and personalise their messages still further. The most famous example of this was Labour's late-night text messages to first-time voters in 2001, highlighting the party's permissive attitude to alcohol licensing reform.

At the same time, there is a widely held view that the main parties have not as yet fully exploited the opportunities offered by digital communications. Admittedly, part of the problem is beyond their control (Ballinger 2002: 230–1). The use of emails and text messages for the purposes of political marketing in the UK is controlled by the Privacy and Electronic Communications (EC Directive) Regulations 2003, which are policed by the Information Commissioner's Office. At the heart of these lies the prior consent rule, which places a considerable limitation on the parties' ability to contact voters by email or text without their consent. The most obvious way to bypass this constraint is to encourage voters to register their contact details online. However, this merely pushes back the problem one level. In a country where fewer than 8 per cent of voters obtain their political information online (Butler and Kavanagh 2006: 169), it follows that, unless they demonstrate remarkable levels of imagination, parties will face an uphill struggle to accumulate vast quantities of personal data via this route. Though it is possible for parties to purchase email addresses in bulk from commercial databases which do comply with the Regulations, they are reluctant to do so on cost grounds, a point which also restricts the transmission of text messages. Ballinger also detects a certain wariness on the part of campaign managers (2002: 230–1). There is a risk that cold calling of this type will be seen by

Box 3.2 Left on the net

Despite having a website since the mid-1990s, the Labour party's presence on the net has been routinely criticised. In one sense, Labour's site includes all of the features one might expect: *Labour. central* enables members and supporters to exchange information; *Labour.vision* links visitors to Labour's page on YouTube and allows for interactive participation with ministers; whilst *Labourspace. com* provides assistance for supporters wishing to develop their own campaigns. Nonetheless, the official site has been criticised for failing to give visitors meaningful opportunities to determine its content, something which experts insist is a *sine qua non* for successful web-based campaigning.

Disaffection with the Labour party's official website has led to two grass-roots initiatives, designed to make good its alleged deficiencies. The first of these, called *LabourHome*, dates from June 2006. Established by Alex Hilton, this site was conceived as a rival to *ConservativeHome*. However, in July 2008, amidst various criticisms of its format, it was purchased by the publishers of the left-wing weekly *The New Statesman*. One of the principal failings, or so it was alleged, was that it failed to offer an independent, 'bottom-up' campaigning forum. In turn, this led a second group of activists, led by former Mandelson aide Derek Draper, to establish *LabourList* in January 2009. This was conceived as a policy-focused site, which would give visitors the opportunity to express their views across the full range of public policy. However, its impact was blunted when Draper, together with Gordon Brown's spin doctor Damien McBride, was implicated in plans for an anti-Tory gossip site to be named *Red Rag*. As a result, McBride resigned his post at Number Ten on 11 April 2009, with Draper stepping down from LabourList on 6 May 2009.

Conservative critics argue that these developments reflect the ongoing failure of Labour supporters to establish sites to rival *ConservativeHome* and *Guido Fawkes*, the irreverent and largely anti-Labour gossip site run by Paul Staines. It was, of course, the latter's success in lampooning senior Labour politicians which encouraged Draper and McBride in their ill-starred Red Rag initiative.

(*Source:* Dale 2009; Sparrow 2009)

Table 3.2 Traffic figures for the websites of the major parties (August 2007)	
Party	Percentage of total internet traffic
British National Party	0.0022
Conservative Party	0.001
Labour Party	0.00051
Liberal Democrats	0.00043
Greens	0.00012

(*Source:* Colville 2008)

some recipients as intrusive and could have the very opposite effect to that intended.

The result is that parties have been content to send digital messages only to those voters who have been prepared to register with them via their websites and it is in relation to this aspect of their digital communications that the main parties have been most heavily criticised. Put simply, the parties are accused of doing remarkably little to 'pull' voters into their virtual domains. Some criticisms have concentrated on technical failures such as website design or a lack of imagination in exploiting search engines. However, the principal criticism is a more fundamental one: parties still have not escaped from the grip of the 'push' technologies and continue to use the digital world 'for information sending rather than interaction – talking at rather than to voters' (Budge et al. 2007: 325). The significance of this criticism hinges on the word 'interaction'. Critics of the parties' approach insist that digital technology has generated its own culture, in which individual users expect to feel in control. Colville (2008: 20–1) quotes one industry insider with telling effect:

> The web . . . is about the users and not editors. The former group are always stranger and more diverse than the latter ever give them credit for. The most you can do on the web is provide a place where they like to gather. You're the hosts and it's your place but you don't really make the rules.

The same source also observes that, to be sustainable among users, the staff managing a website should not aim to provide more than 5 per cent of the material. This point is echoed by those who have established alternative sites to compensate for the weaknesses of the official sites (Colville 2008: 8; Dale 2009). If true, it may also go some way to explain why the latter receive so little traffic.

Lessons from America

These criticisms have been thrown into even shaper relief by the 2008 US Presidential elections. This is not simply because key players made so much use of the internet, including their own personal websites, during the campaign. More importantly, Barack Obama in particular used digital communication to revive local campaigning in ways which badly exposed the failure of UK parties to understand the different mentality the internet in particular encourages its users to adopt.

The '50 state strategy' and mybarackobama.com

In 2004, Democrat Senator Howard Dean briefly shocked American pundits with his use of digital communications to support his bid for the Democrat nomination. Not only did Dean use his website to raise funds, but he also ensured that it linked visitors to social networking sites (most notably Meetup.com) frequented by other Dean supporters, the hope being that they would use the latter to plan locally based pro-Dean campaign events. As things transpired, however, this was not enough to secure for Dean the Democratic nomination.

However, Dean subsequently used his experiences to devise for the Democrat party as a whole what became known as the '50 state strategy'. For a number of years the Democrats had been concerned about the ability of the Republicans to mobilise support at grass-roots level via a nationwide network of influential and pro-Republican opinion-formers, often linked to local churches. Dean's belief was that the Democrats had to rival these Republican tactics and that the internet, especially the social networking sites, offered the best means of doing so.

Aside from the highly ambitious – and controversial – decision to spread campaign resources across the entire USA, the most striking feature of Dean's strategy was its use of the internet as the primary organisational tool. The '50 state strategy' worked by the central recruitment and training of Democrat activists who, armed with the latest web-based techniques, would be sent back to their own neighbourhoods to build campaign organisations at that level. The internet was particularly useful as a means of 'pulling' otherwise non-committed voters into the campaign, both by encouraging them to contribute financially (even the smallest amounts being happily accepted) and with opinions and ideas.

Barack Obama's presidential campaign built upon these developments via his website mybarackobama.com. According to McElhatton (2008), the central feature of this site was the way in which it 'harnessed all the best attributes of social media' by encouraging volunteers to discuss online how they could campaign for Obama in their own communities. This was reinforced by a number of innovative technological applications:

- A facility was added to mybarackobama.com so that users could customise it to suit their own preferences
- Website managers worked furiously to ensure that the content was updated as often as possible in a bid to keep users entertained and motivated.
- An application was made available to iPhone users enabling them to find the nearest Obama campaign offices and events, as well as providing a further opportunity to make campaign donations.
- The official Obama website established multiple links to 30 social networking sites in order to create the widest possible digital presence and in the process emphasise the number of people interested in his campaign.
- This was complemented by an unprecedented use of text messaging. By the end of the campaign, over one million voters were receiving text messages, something which Sarachan (2009) argues was an important and underestimated element of the campaign not least because it meant that messages could be sent to a generation of voters used to communicating on the move.

Perhaps the most remarkable technological aspect of the Obama campaign was that it evolved in ways that surprised his staff (McCormick 2009). This was especially true of the mobile telephone applications. However, from a political perspective its most important feature was the way in which mybarackobama.com was transformed from a traditional 'gatekeeper', via which corporate messages could be pushed out to the electorate, to a trusted resource, which gave local activists a sense of personal ownership of the Obama brand. Sarachan (2009) refers to this group as 'brand evangelists' and argues that, just had Dean had foreseen, they used their personal contacts to interpret and spread the Obama message in what she calls ever wider 'concentric circles' of marketing. The *Washington Post* estimated that as many as 200,000 offline events were organised via social networking sites, Twitter being particularly important. The fact that these evangelists have 'the built-in trust and ability to influence other stakeholders' means that they can reach the electorate in ways which the most sophisticated marketing exercise cannot hope to match. This reinforces the importance of constantly updating the campaign messages via a multitude of social networking sites and text messaging. The latter in particular have the capacity to engage the evangelists as they go about their daily lives – hence extending still further their capacity to spread the message to others. Little wonder that the Obama campaign was described as 'the biggest mobile and social media campaign in history', whose central features are likely to shape party political communication the world over (McCormick 2009).

Conclusion: a note of caution

It is easy to exaggerate the impact of Obama's digital campaign or indeed the extent to which Dean's strategy actually contributed to Obama's victory. In the first place, the 2008 Presidential election was not simply a digital contest. McElhatton (2008) insists that campaigners used the 'widest possible mix of offline and online media' and, further, quotes a number of experts to the effect that traditional advertising and public relations still have a part to play in political marketing, especially in an era which has witnessed the collapse of meaningful ideological distinctions between the main parties. McElhatton also suggests that the unprecedented $600 million Obama was able to raise in campaign funds played an indispensible part in employing the campaign managers needed to run the online part of his operations.

At the same time, there is little doubt that the Dean and, later,

Obama campaigns point to some hugely significant developments in local campaigning. Most important of these are the notions that local activists using the latest digital technologies can revive old-style retail politics and that, once they have completed their training programmes, this local cadre should be left largely to its own devices. Whilst this chimes perfectly with the culture of the digital natives, it is nonetheless a revolutionary development for national campaign managers brought up in the Millbank era. They might argue (and with some justice) that the success of the Obama online campaign was the product of uniquely North American circumstances, which will not lend themselves to easy transfer to the UK. However, whilst this may be true, one thing remains certain: if they wish to exploit fully the considerable advantages offered by digital technology, British parties will have to take a leaf from the Obama book – and sooner rather than later.

 What you should have learnt from reading this chapter

- The reasons why national campaigning may be less successful in the post-modern era.

- Why targeting emerged as a key feature of communication strategies and the extent to which targeting operations have become so much more sophisticated.

- How and why direct marketing has replaced pre-modern retail politics.

- Why UK parties have been accused of an unsatisfactory response to the advent of digital communications.

- How constituency campaigning has changed during the modern era and how the latter is likely to change still further as a result of developments in the USA.

 Glossary of key terms

Battleground constituencies These are the constituencies party strategists believe are most likely to change hands at the next election. Inevitably, therefore, they will dominate the parties' targeting operations.
'New' working class An umbrella term to describe the fragmentation of lifestyle and attitude within the working class. The 'new' working class was composed of more skilled manual workers, who lived in or aspired to live in homes they actually owned and had little sympathy for the trade unionism and high public spending historically associated with the Labour party.

Likely examination questions

Why do some commentators argue that centralised national campaigns have lost much of their effectiveness?

Explain the nature and purpose of both targeting and direct marketing in party political communication.

In what ways and to what extent have recent developments both at home and abroad exposed a serious failure among UK political parties to adapt to digital communications?

Helpful websites

The main parties all have their own websites, which offer a range of information and other services. The Labour party can be found at www.labour.org.uk, which includes a section on blogs and a multimedia portal which enables one to surf a variety of speeches and podcasts. As is well known, the Conservatives have recently invested heavily in a new site (www.conservatives.com), the centrepiece of which is 'Webcameron' with links to David Cameron's diary, speeches and videos. The Liberal Democrats site is www.libdems.org.uk, the Scottish National Party www.snp.org and the Democratic Unionists www.dup.org.uk. In addition, some of the unofficial sites can be found at http://conservativehome.blogs.com, www.labourhome.org and www.labourlist.org.

Suggestions for further reading

An excellent summary of the recent evolution of constituency campaigning can be found in J. Fisher at al., *Constituency Campaigning in the 2005 British General Election*, which can be found at www.essex.ac.uk/. . ./ EPOPPaperforFisheretal.doc. A very useful introduction to the new media can be found in Chapter 10 of Ralph Negrine's *Politics and the Mass Media in Britain* (Abingdon: Routledge, 1994). Stephen Coleman's 'Online Campaigning' in P. Norris (ed.), *Britain Votes 2001* (Oxford: Oxford University Press, 2001) covers the role of the New Media in the 2001 general election. Robert Colville's *Politics, Policy and the Internet* offers invaluable insight into the UK parties' response to digital communications and can be found at www.cps.org.uk.

Political Advertising

Contents

Overview

Chapter 4 examines how communication strategists use advertising to sell political parties to the electorate. After summarising how political advertising is designed to work, this chapter goes on to identify the main features of the legal regime which controls the placement of advertisements, this being the one area of party political communications which is heavily controlled by statute. Thereafter, it explores the principal mechanisms of political advertising in an attempt to explain how marketing experts aim to maximise their impact. The final section concentrates on the apparent paradox running through political advertising: despite the vast amounts of money devoted to it, there remain considerable doubts over its impact on voters.

Key issues to be covered in this chapter

- The theory underpinning political advertising
- The legal restrictions on the placement of political advertisements
- The changing nature of both party political broadcasts and paid-for adverts
- The arguments for a new regulatory regime
- The debate over the value and effectiveness of political advertising

The theory of advertising

In the 1950s, US advertising executives, led by the legendary figure of Rosser Reeves, began to argue that the techniques used to market ordinary commercial products could be used also to 'sell' politics. Their faith in the power of advertising was rooted in the lessons the industry was rapidly learning about human psychology. By far the most important of these was the implausibility of selling a product by a literal representation of its internal qualities. This was especially so when a wide and largely undifferentiated range of products – soap powders being the obvious example – were competing for the same market. Instead, the product's utility had to be augmented by what McNair (2007: 88) refers to as a sign-value. Essentially, this meant that images and signs external to the product, but familiar to the target audiences, would be transferred to the product in the hope that they would add to its consumer value. The great skill of advertisers was to establish precisely which images would most effectively achieve this and how best to 'load' them on to the product. In turn, this demanded a detailed understanding of consumers: what it is they want from a product and why.

Today, the ultimate goal of the advertising industry is to create what is known as a brand. This happens when consumers associate a product so strongly with their values and desires that their attachment to it becomes automatic. There may be in fact very little difference between their preferred brand and other products. However, that is not how they will see matters. For them, their brand's usefulness is measured far more by what it represents than what it actually does. So powerful is this image that it will invariably ensure brand loyalty, regardless of the availability of alternatives.

This feature of the brand is particularly pertinent to the world of politics, where the pioneers of psychographics – Dick Wirthlin and Roger Ailes – not only discovered the importance of personal values as a determinant of voting behavior, but also the extent to which the former are rooted in powerful myths and symbols (McNair 2007: 94). It is little wonder, therefore, that when they discovered the seminal importance of the so-called **American dream** for Republican voters, Wirthlin and Ailes advised Ronald Reagan to base his own political messages around the values widely associated with the

'Founding Fathers'. In this way, Reagan was able to persuade millions of US voters of very modest means to endorse sweeping tax cuts, even though they themselves would not be the principal beneficiaries.

Political advertising in the UK

The faith of US politicians in the claims of advertisers eventually influenced the attitudes of their British counterparts. At the same time, it is important to remember that, unlike the situation in the USA, British practices are severely constrained by electoral law. In addition to the severe spending limits on individual candidates, parties are prevented from placing any paid-for advertisements on the broadcast media. This principle was originally established with the foundation of the BBC and was reaffirmed during the parliamentary debates on commercialising television in the early 1950s. It is now enshrined in statute via the 2003 Communications Act.

By way of compensation, a dual system of political broadcasts was established to give campaign managers at least some of the television exposure they craved. This is also a notable departure from US practice and helps give political advertising in the UK its distinctive characteristics. As we shall see below, however, it places an important question mark over the extent to which political advertising can be as successful in Britain as it has been in the US (McNair 2007: 88).

Political broadcasts

Political broadcasts come in two forms: party political broadcasts (PPBs) and party election broadcasts (PEBs). Though they are not paid-for advertisements in the standard sense of that term, commentators still classify them as such on the grounds that

> they are produced using the same techniques and with the same budgets as commercial advertisers and offer the politicians who commission them the same degree of editorial control. In their televisual format, they are also the nearest the UK comes to the 'TV spot' adverts which dominate political advertising in the USA. (Franklin 2004: 121)

PPBs are allocated to parties on an annual basis, regardless of whether or not an election campaign has been scheduled. Self-evidently, PEBs are available only during an official campaign. The first party broadcasts date from 1924 though it was not until 1929 that the first bespoke PEB was made. A host of technological and political factors determined that it would be another 22 years before the first televised broadcast – for the Liberal party – was made, on 15 October 1951.

The allocation of party broadcasts

For years the allocation of party broadcasts was the preserve of the Committee on Party Political Broadcasting, on which representatives of the major parties were joined by executives from the main broadcast organisations. However, the negotiations which took place prior to the 1983 general election were so unpleasant that the broadcasters ruled that future discussions would take place on an informal basis via the Chief Whip's Office. Even so, all the evidence suggests that the parties continue to vigorously defend their positions. This is not necessarily because broadcasts have an intrinsic marketing value. More importantly, the allocation of PEBs is used by the broadcasters as a yardstick to determine how much news coverage each party is entitled to. The current allocation of PEBs can be gleaned from Table 4.1.

The changing content and format of televisual broadcasts

Almost inevitably, the content and format of televisual broadcasts have changed considerably. The first major innovation came in 1959 when Labour used a magazine format based on the BBC's popular current affairs programme *Tonight*. As a result, its broadcasts were fast-moving and used a sequence of film reports, animations, interviews and celebrity testimonials. However, in the years which followed it was the Conservative party which set new standards for imaginative and innovative broadcasting. Their 1970 general election campaign was particularly important in this respect. Conservative publicity director Geoffrey Tucker used PEBs extensively to 'humanise' party leader Edward Heath. He also commissioned a PEB dealing directly with one of the Conservatives' key campaign messages, the impact of inflation on the purchasing power of working-class women, a work which attracted considerable media attention by being the first to star an 'ordinary' person. Yet Tucker's real innovation was in insisting

Table 4.1 Televised party election broadcasts and the 2005 general election

Party	Broadcast 1	Broadcast 2	Broadcast 3	Broadcast 4	Broadcast 5
Labour	Monday 11 April	Friday 15 April	Tuesday 19 April	Wednesday 27 April	Tuesday 3 May
Conservatives	Tuesday 12 April	Saturday 16 April	Wednesday 20 April	Saturday 30 April	Monday 2 May
Lib Dems	Wednesday 13 April	Sunday 17 April	Monday 25 April	Sunday 1 May	
SNP	Thursday 14 April	Monday 18 April	Sunday 24 April		
Plaid Cymru	Thursday 14 April	Tuesday 19 April	Friday 22 April		
Greens	Tuesday 28 April				
Socialist Labour	Friday 29 April				
Scottish Socialists	Friday 22 April				
UKIP	Friday 29 April				
BNP	Tuesday 21 April				

that the Conservatives recruit a team of experts to make the broadcasts and give them unprecedented latitude to make full use their talents. Unsurprisingly, this resulted in a series of wonderfully shot and edited films, replete with very striking but negative images: the '**ten bob pound**' and a literally frozen pay packet.

These innovations subsequently provided the perfect platform for **Tim Bell** and Saatchi and Saatchi – the legendary advertising company given responsibility for all aspects of Conservative publicity in March 1978 – to take political broadcasting to an altogether new level. For Rosenbaum (1997: 59), the great strength of the Saatchis' material was to draw on US influences and transform the PEB into a political commercial, hallmarked by 'faster cutting, the use of professional actors, more special effects, more imaginative and dramatic devices, and the reduction of talking politicians to a bare minimum.' Whilst their efforts were not always successful, the ill-starred 1987 general election campaign being the most notable example, few could doubt the professionalism of the Saatchi product, nor the fact that it was so obviously rooted in the news values of the day. This was certainly true of the length of a typical Saatchi broadcast, which rarely exceeded half of the duration of earlier efforts.

The agency justified these changes by pointing out that the abolition of fixed-time transmission meant that, for the first time, the broadcasts had to compete with other programmes for viewers' attentions. However, this did not prevent the new-style broadcasts coming in for increasing criticism, in particular that they were too emotional, too sensational and, above all, 'unrelentingly negative' (Franklin 2004: 124). At the same time it should be pointed out that the Saatchis' innovations were soon copied by the other parties. This was most obviously so in the case of the Labour party, whose broadcasts also made great use of the biopic and fictional narratives, a trend which peaked with 'Kinnock: the movie' in 1987 (see below) and the emotional and highly controversial '**Jennifer's ear**' broadcast of 24 March 1992.

The other great change to occur to political broadcasting followed a consultation exercise conducted by the broadcasters themselves in 1998. As a result, it was agreed that the historic five- and ten-minute slots would be replaced by three shorter alternatives, lasting

Box 4.1 The impact of the Saatchis on political broadcasting

- Broadcasts were radically reduced in length so as to bring them into line with ordinary commercial spots
- The content became much more irreverent, even 'tongue in cheek'
- Politicians were increasingly replaced by actors
- Voice-over techniques were used more frequently
- Personality dominated politics
- Appeals were made to emotion rather than reason
- The format increasingly aped that of ordinary television programmes
- Most importantly, regardless of whether a party was in opposition or office, the strategy was the same: attack the opposition with negative copy

(*Source:* Franklin 2004: 123)

Box 4.2 The biopic

The award for the most well-received PEB in recent years – and the competition is not great – goes to Hugh Hudson's 1987 'biopic' of Neil Kinnock, which was devised by Labour's campaign managers as a means of buttressing Kinnock's reputation as a deeply empathetic human being. The effect on his personal ratings was dramatic: an immediate increase of sixteen percentage points among those who saw the broadcast. Unfortunately, since only one quarter of voters fell into this category, the broadcast did little to transform Labour's electoral fortunes. Despite this, 'Kinnock: the movie' was hugely influential among politicians and was shamelessly copied by the Conservatives five years later. Sean Woodward, then head of Conservative publicity, hired an even more famous director to commit the story of John Major's life to celluloid. The late John Schlesinger's *The Journey* duly charted Major's rise from the streets of Brixton to the premiership.

4 minutes and 40 seconds, 3 minutes and 40 seconds, and 2 minutes and 40 seconds respectively. Unsurprisingly given that they had been complaining for some time that broadcasts were too long, the latter soon became the parties' overwhelming choice.

The changing purpose of political broadcasting and the debate reform

Ultimately, these changes reflect the fact that the *purpose* of party broadcasts has evolved quite considerably since they were first produced in the 1920s. Most obviously, they no longer make any attempt to educate and persuade but 'to place issues on news and campaign agendas' (Franklin 2004: 121), a point with which they have much in common with the other forms of political advertising. This fact, together with the opprobrium heaped on the actual content, begs the question: why has political broadcasting not been reformed? This is particularly puzzling given that the Electoral Commission has commented favourably on their continuing importance. However, whilst the Commission has accepted that the length of broadcasts can be reduced further still, to 1 minute and 30 seconds, it is adamant that the existing system remains more or less intact.

The most obvious option would be to amend the 2003 Communications Act and permit the parties to pay for political commercials as is the case in the USA. Despite the fact that such a proposal would meet with massive opposition, there are three important arguments in its favour:

- Research data from the US suggests that a series of 30- to 60-second 'spots', frequently repeated, would bring numerous benefits to the effectiveness of political communication (Franklin 2004: 124–5).
- Allowing the parties to buy advertising space from broadcasters would enable them to produce a new generation of PEBs transmitted via the 'narrowcast' digital media.
- Reform would go some way to neutralise the enormous advantages given to the party of government, which can advertise its policies on television at public expense whilst denying this privilege to its rivals (McNair 2007: 113).

For the moment, however, the critics of paid-for 'spots' remain unconvinced. The case against radical reform is almost certainly influenced by British perceptions of US practices, in particular the fear that their introduction would trivialise and personalise politics, encourage negative campaigning, manipulate the electorate and strengthen still further the political advantages of the well-financed.

Table 4.2 The penetration of party election broadcasts (figures as percentage of the electorate)		
Election	**Saw television PEBs**	**Heard radio PEBs**
1997	73	15
2001	58	16
2005	70	20

(*Source:* Butler and Kavanagh 1997: 217; Ballinger 2002: 214; Butler and Kavanagh 2006: 169)

Readers are invited to draw their own conclusions whether the emergence of such negative phenomena would constitute a major departure from current British practice.

Paid-for advertising

This is the second and much older source of political advertising. A particularly important departure occurred immediately after World War I, when the Conservatives first used the services of advertising agencies, a practice soon followed by their rivals. Thereafter, the format of paid-for advertising has not changed greatly, with the main parties still opting for a combination of poster sites and newspaper space for what is invariably cleverly designed and sometimes even amusing copy.

Certain developments are visible. One of these is a series of changes to the timing of the advertisements. This sequence began in June 1957 when **Colman Prentis Varley** (CPV) devised the first 'long campaign' for the Conservatives. Their rationale, which was undoubtedly influenced by the parties' failure to appreciate their changed legal position, was to expose target voters to a sustained period of advertising *two years or so before* they went to the polls, advertising then being terminated once the official campaign period began. This 'slow burn' approach set the trend for the next 17 years, only to change abruptly in February 1974 when the Liberal party finally exploited the *Tronah Mines* ruling by running an advertisement in the *Daily Express* eight days after the general election had been

Table 4.3 Political advertising in national daily and weekly newspapers (general elections only)

Party	Number of pages				
	1987	1992	1997	2001	2005
Conservatives	217	48	27	0	4
Labour	202	65	12.5	7	22
Lib Dems	17	6.5	0.2	0	8.9
Other parties	0.1	42	13.2	5	0

(*Source:* Nuffield Studies 1987–2005)

called. Thereafter, whilst the parties have not abandoned the long campaign altogether, they have devoted more of their advertising resources to 'sudden and intense activity once the election is called . . . [which] usually culminates in a final blitz in the last week or ten days' (Rosenbaum 1997: 31). The resulting scramble for advertising billboards, in particular, is often a manic affair. This was certainly the case in early spring 2001, when the general election was postponed owing to the foot-and-mouth crisis. The two major parties were subsequently forced to sell on their prime sites before repurchasing them for the end of May.

A second development concerns the parties' choice of advertising media. Despite doubts about their cost-effectiveness (Franklin 2004: 129), newspaper advertisements had been the medium of choice, culminating in the unprecedented expenditure on newspaper advertising during the 1987 general election. However, by the time the nation went to the polls again five years later, Conservative and Labour spending on newspaper advertising had effectively halved (Rosenbaum 1997: 33). The main casualty was the national press, something which almost certainly reflects parties' concern over declining newspaper circulation, the lack of campaign coverage in the more popular papers and the fragmentation of the media as a result of the digital revolution. The shift in advertising away from the national press is also influenced by the prominence of the parties'

Table 4.4 Voters having seen billboard advertisements (figures as percentages of sample)			
Year	Labour party sites	Conservative party sites	All sites
1997	55	53	70
2001	35	31	50

(*Source:* Franklin 2004: 130–1)

targeting strategies. Fisher et al. (2005) note that the lion's share of the advertising spend is now concentrated on the purchase of poster sites on key locations within each target constituency, supported by advertisements in the local and regional titles. This also helps explain the apparent paradox whereby, despite the shift in resources, the number of voters reporting to have seen billboard advertisements has actually decreased.

Advertising copy
As is the case with political broadcasting, however, the most significant changes have occurred to advertising copy. The celebrated CPV campaign between 1957 and 1959 is an obvious case in point. The Conservatives' communications strategy was based on presenting themselves 'as champions of prosperity and opportunities for ordinary families' (Rosenbaum 1997: 7). However, rather than use the traditional techniques to support such an apolitical, family-friendly message, CPV copy substituted photographs of leading Tory politicians, text and political jargon with positive images of ordinary people. These images were clearly designed to associate rising prosperity with the Conservative party, pretty standard fare for the commercial world but unprecedented in UK politics until this point.

The next – and still dominant - phase in the development of advertising copy built upon this by substituting positive images of the party commissioning the advertisement for negative images of its opponents. Once again, this strategy was rooted in opinion research, which continues to show that the most memorable copy is that which rubbishes the opposition. The key election was 1970, when

Box 4.3 Labour and Conservative party choice of advertising agencies in UK general elections

Party	1992	1997	2001	2005	2010
Conserv-atives	Saatchi and Saatchi	Saatchi and Saatchi	Yellow M	Immediate Sales	Euro RSCG
Labour	Shadow Commu-nications Agency	BMP	TBWA	TBWA	Saatchi and Saatchi

the Conservatives' copy focused strongly on the failings of Labour's economic management and its impact on working-class families. (This complemented the famous series of PEBs discussed in the previous section.) The Tory copy drew a furious response from Labour, whose 'Yesterday's men' advertisement of 14 April is described by Rosenbaum (1997: 11) as 'the first really dramatic . . . "attack" political advertisement'.

These developments set the scene for the Saatchis to make their own unique contribution seven years later. The copy they produced for the Conservative party was some of the most famous witnessed in Britain, taking belligerent and negative advertising to a new level. The Saatchis' material was based on the simple premise that the key sections of the electorate were deeply unhappy with the Labour party. It did not matter, therefore, whether the Conservatives were in opposition (as in 1979) or defending their record in government (as in 1983): in either scenario, Labour would be attacked remorselessly. This is not to denigrate the quality of the Saatchis' copy. At the same time, this does not disguise the fact that its most innovative feature was the way in which it downgraded its client in order to concentrate on the perceived failings of its opponents. This was particularly noticeable in 1983, when the Conservatives campaigned as a de facto opposition party in order to concentrate on their prime electoral asset: the unelectable nature of Michael Foot's Labour party.

Thereafter, negative copy has come to dominate paid-for advertising. Nor is it the case that the Conservatives have a monopoly on controversy. In 2005, for example, Labour got itself into some trouble over images on its website of the infamous Shakespearian character Shylock. The principal targets were Howard and shadow chancellor Oliver Letwin, both Jewish.

Running battles: advertisers and politicians

The growing negativity of advertising copy has generated considerable tension within the political parties. This is exemplified by the row which broke out between the Conservative party and the Saatchis in 1996–7. Unsurprisingly, the most controversial advertisement was the portrayal of Blair as a ventriloquist's dummy sitting on German Chancellor Helmut Kohl's knees, copy which reflected the Saatchi's insistence that attacking Blair personally offered the best hope of undermining Labour's lead. John Major felt that the advertisement was beneath the dignity of his party, whilst his aides questioned whether the agency had properly researched the copy. Brian Mawhinney, then the Conservative party chairman, subsequently ordered his own officials to test subsequent copy, only to discover that the negative advertisements tested particularly well. Interestingly, fearing that the research findings would fail to convince John Major, Mawhinney nevertheless ordered the harder-hitting material to be pulled.

This episode reflects a deeper tension between politicians and advertising agencies. It has manifested itself on numerous occasions over the last 40 years and has its roots both in politicians' egos and a marked difference in priorities.

* Firstly, politicians – especially the more successful ones – continue to struggle to accept that copywriters have the better insight into the minds of voters. This tension is at its greatest when campaign polling fails to reveal signs of electoral recovery. As a result, politicians are invariably encouraged to reject professional advice and, as the Conservative leadership did in 1997, insist on adopting their own copy.
* Secondly, they instinctively wish to advertise their own achievements and beliefs rather than the failings of their opponents. This was famously the case in 1987, when Margaret Thatcher objected to the Saatchis' negative approach so strongly that the

Conservatives' campaign was very nearly derailed. However, Labour insiders also record how the 1997 campaign was marred by Blair's unease over the negative nature of Labour's copy. At his insistence, Labour produced a series of posters on single campaign themes, linked by the overarching slogan 'Britain Deserves Better'. In the end, however, the professionals got their way: Labour's final advertisement in 1997 was very negative, with images of Major and Clarke portrayed as Laurel and Hardy set against the slogan 'Another Five Years? Another Fine Mess.'

- Thirdly, politicians habitually 'watch the purse strings'. Consequently, as soon as they believe that a contest has been effectively won, they will axe campaign budgets and with it some of the most expensive copy. A very prominent example of this was Cecil Parkinson's decision to scrap the Saatchis' three-page 'If . . .' newspaper ad in 1983, despite the agency's insistence that it was among its best-ever copy (Kavanagh 1995: 61).

Political advertising: an evaluation and appraisal

In his own study of political communication, McNair (2007: 87) places advertising alongside public relations as the two most important means of delivering political messages. However, whilst this is undoubtedly true, it does not necessarily mean that advertising is particularly effective in influencing political opinion. On the contrary, the statistical evidence in Table 4.5, drawn from the responses of voters themselves, strongly suggests that both PEBs and paid-for advertising are widely disregarded. This section examines this proposition in more detail, largely by looking at the views of academic commentators.

The power of television broadcasts

The theoretical advantage of party broadcasts in particular should not be underestimated. Crucially, they remain 'the one occasion when the parties address voters with no external intervention' (Butler and Kavanagh 2006: 111). Further advantages include:

- The capacity to help bring coherence to the communication strategy

	Great deal	Fair amount	Not very much	None at all	Don't know	Rating
Table 4.5 The relative persuasiveness of political advertising						
PEBs on TV	6	16	20	57	1	–55
Billboard advertisements	2	8	17	72	1	–79
Election coverage on TV	13	36	20	30	1	–1
Election coverage in newspapers	8	30	22	39	1	–23

(*Source:* Ballinger 2002: 215; MORI/Election Commission)

• The opportunity to deal with specific issues
• The unique marketing value they offer the minor parties, who rarely receive promotional opportunities of a comparable nature.

A good example of the last of these points is the decision of the Greens to field 50 candidates in order to qualify for a PEB in 1979. Though it would be a grand overstatement to suggest that this party's fortunes were transformed as a result, equally the exposure they gained was a milestone in the party's development.

Despite these advantages, however, the general consensus is that making effective broadcasts has become harder than ever. There are many reasons for this.

• Whereas they were once the only form of political programme on television during election campaigns, '[n]ow they are a drop in the ocean of political broadcasting' (Rosenbaum 1997: 41).
• They have also suffered from the decision, taken voluntarily by politicians, to drop compulsory simultaneous broadcasts.
• This problem was compounded by the dramatic increase in the number of channels following the Broadcasting Act 1990 – not only can viewers switch from a party broadcast to an alternative, there are now so many of the latter from which to choose.

- Even attempts to counter this problem have merely created new difficulties. At three minutes the modern PEB is one-tenth of the length of its predecessors from the 1920s, something which seriously restricts the editorial latitude of those who make them.

Little wonder, therefore, that Butler and Kavanagh (2006: 111) describe party broadcasts as 'a shrunken shadow of their former selves'. They argue that, in the 2005 general election, only one PEB – Labour's first broadcast on the Blair–Brown relationship – had a measurable impact on the campaign. More importantly still, the reason for this was largely because its content was taken up by the media the following day.

Paid-for advertising

A similar picture emerges in respect of paid-for advertising. Despite the creativity, innovation and cost, there is a marked lack of evidence to support the view that advertising in newspapers and on billboards makes a noticeable difference to political outcomes (Branigan 2006). This is even so when, as was the case with the Conservatives in 1970, the copy itself is widely praised for its innovation and originality (Kavanagh 1995: 54). McNair (2007: 33) confirms that research supports these private findings, adding that the effects of advertisements 'are heavily conditioned by the existing political attitudes of the audience'. In short, it is only when little is known about a candidate or party that an advertisement is likely to make a difference. The consensus among commentators therefore is surely captured by Denis Kavanagh who suggests that 'adverts work when they go with the grain; when they work with something that already exists' (quoted in Branigan 2006).

In other words, whilst adverts may have a reinforcement effect, they cannot place into the public consciousness a completely new idea. Philip Gould acknowledges this when he states that a particularly well-timed advert can capture the wider political mood and remind voters what it is that they are really feeling (1998: 314). He also bluntly dismisses as nonsense any suggestion that good advertising produces election victories. He adds that for advertising to have the capacity of achieving such an effect, it would be necessary to order a sweeping reform of electoral law and permit unlimited paid-for advertising on television in the manner of the US.

Party	Advertising bill (£)	Seats won	Advertising spend per seat gained (£)
Table 4.6 The cost and rewards of political advertising in the 2005 general election (£)			
Conservative	8,175,166	197	41,498
Labour	5,286,997	355	14,893
Liberal Democrat	1,583,058	62	25,533
SNP	40,411	6	6,735

Conclusion

In this chapter we have concentrated on the evolution of political advertising and some of the political and academic controversies which result. Perhaps the most important and surprising question this raises is: why do the parties bother at all with advertising copy? Part of the answer to this might lie in tradition; part in the notion that the electorate expects to see political advertising during a campaign; and that parties which fail to respect this would lose out as a result. Equally, it might be contended that party activists and supporters will also expect to see advertisements, especially in the target constituencies, and draw some sort of inspiration as a result – what Franklin (2004: 129) refers to as heartening the committed and restoring the faith of doubters.

Yet, from the somewhat narrower perspective of effects, it is hard to resist the conclusion that parties are getting precious few returns from their often considerable financial outlays. A particularly interesting item of qualitative evidence to support this is the 'poster ad'. This is, quite literally, a single poster, which is placed in neither newspapers nor on billboards. Instead, it is unveiled before the media at the morning election press conference on the assumption that newspaper and television broadcast editors will use shots in their own election coverage. For Franklin (2004: 129), the poster ad is also the clearest evidence of the changing function of political advertising. Whereas it once genuinely aimed to persuade, now it aims instead 'to create news and gain television coverage for the party'. In the same study, he goes on to add that 'the propaganda weapons of posters, newspaper adverts and PEBs are of secondary importance' compared to the techniques of news management which form 'the heart of parties' communications campaigns' (Franklin 2004: 132). Consequently, it is to these techniques and, more importantly, what it is that parties hope to gain from them, that we must now turn.

. . . .

 What you should have gained from reading this chapter

- A clearer insight into the theory of advertising.

- How parties use both political broadcasting and paid-for advertising to sell themselves to voters.

- Why it is argued that the law governing political broadcasting should be reformed.

- Why politicians are often dissatisfied with the quality of political advertising.

- The reasons why a major question mark hangs over the effectiveness of political advertising.

Glossary of key terms

American dream A term which refers to the enduring myth that the USA remains the land of opportunity and that, through hard work and self-reliance, even the most humble citizen can acquire extraordinary wealth and prominence.

Tim Bell The leading Saatchi executive who handled the Conservatives' account for much of Lady Thatcher's time as party leader. He had a particularly strong relationship with Thatcher, who valued his services as a media adviser more than any other. He was knighted in 1990 and ennobled eight years later.

Colman Prentis Varley (CPV) The name of a legendary London advertising agency, whose work for the Conservative party in the 1950s ushered in a new era in the history of political advertising.

Jennifer's ear A popular term – playing on the eighteenth-century Anglo-Spanish War of Jenkins' Ear – which was used by journalists to describe the political furore which broke out after the broadcast in 1992 of a Labour PEB attacking the Conservative government's record on health care.

Ten bob pound A popular Conservative soundbite from the 1970 general election, which was used to draw voters' attention to the declining purchasing power of sterling as a result of Labour's alleged economic mismanagement. In fact, there were actually 20 shillings to the pound.

 ## Likely examination questions

In what ways and to what effect have political parties in the UK used advertising to support their communication strategies?

Discuss the arguments for and against the proposition that the parties should be able to purchase advertising 'spots' on television?

Why is political advertising so controversial?

 ## Helpful websites

The Advertising Standards Authority, which has information on the legal regime governing the placement of political adverts, is located at www.asa.org.uk. The Open Democracy forum, whose work covers the impact of political advertising (and other forms of political communication) on democracy in the UK and elsewhere can be found at www.opendemocracy.net.

Further reading

A variety of textbooks offer valuable coverage of political advertising. The post-war history of advertising is covered by Chapter 1 of Rosenbaum's 1997 study. More recent developments are assessed in Chapter 6 of Bob Franklin's *Packaging Politics* (London: Hodder Arnold, 2004) and Chapter 6 of Brian McNair's *An Introduction to Political Communications* (Oxford: Routledge, 2007).

News Management: the Rise of the Spin Doctor

Contents

Overview

The resistance of the electorate to their propaganda has resulted in political parties shifting the main thrust of their campaigning to the media. In turn, this has seen the emergence of a new category of media professional: the publicity and press officer, more commonly known as the spin doctor. Chapter 5 is chiefly an examination of the techniques the latter have developed to gain control over the all-important news agenda. In addition, it will also explore some of the main collateral developments, most notably the rise of image management and its implications for intra-party democracy.

Key issues to be covered in this chapter

- Why and how parties seek to 'make' the news
- The role and techniques of the spin doctor in news management
- The value of media monitoring and rebuttal
- The importance of personal and collective image management and its implications for internal party discipline

Making the news

Communicating via the media offers various advantages to political parties. Aside from the fact that news coverage is happily consumed by millions of people each day, their messages can also gain in both credibility and impact because of the perceived independence of the carrier. The downside, however, is the effective surrender of control of the *end use* of their propaganda to people – journalists and their editors – over whose constancy and morality they have the gravest reservations. Often bitter experience has told the parties that merely placing messages before the media in the hope that the latter will pick them up is not enough. If it is to be effective, mediated communication has to be relentlessly proactive.

Feeding the pack: press conferences and pseudo-events

Being proactive means helping journalists make the news. The latter must have something to report. Unless the parties provide them with copy, they will simply go elsewhere to find it. Further, the nature of the copy they offer has to be adapted to the ways in which the modern media actually functions, the best being brief, simple, consistent and, above all, visual (Rosenbaum 1997: 85). This realisation dawned in the late 1950s, when election speeches were timed to coincide with the evening news broadcasts (Rosenbaum 1997: 82). Thereafter, the drive to 'make the headlines' has grown exponentially, culminating in the emergence of the highly sophisticated communications and message grids discussed in Chapter 2. The grids combine to bring remarkable levels of order and structure to election campaigning. More importantly, they form the trough from which the media 'pack' can feed.

The sequence begins with the daily, morning press conference. Aside from allowing the parties to announce their day's campaign theme, press conferences also enable them to exploit the overnight work undertaken by researchers. A large part of the conference, as a result, will be given over to rebutting the anticipated attacks of their opponents and, better still, drawing the media's attention to the latter's own difficulties. The morning press conference is aimed directly at the lunchtime television news bulletins. Though broadcasting regulations guarantee the main parties equal coverage, it is

Box 5.1 The sequence of press conferences during the 1997 general election

Liberal Democrats
This party began the daily sequence. The approach of the Liberal Democrats was as follows:

- 6.00 a.m.   Initial preparatory meeting
- 7.00 a.m.   Final preparatory meeting
- *8.00 a.m.*   *Daily press conference*
- 10.00 a.m.   Campaign meeting
- 5.30 p.m.   Second campaign meeting
- 10.00 p.m.   Briefing with leader Paddy Ashdown

Labour
The Labour party sought to maximise the advantage accruing from its extensive (and expensive) campaign team assembled in Millbank. The essence of Labour's approach was to maintain a 24-hour news-management operation during the campaign.

- 1.00 a.m.   'Daily brief' faxed to all candidates in anticipation of the daily press conference 7.5 hours later
- 7.00 a.m.   Preparatory meeting/final daily campaign planning meeting
- *8.30 a.m.*   *Daily press conference*
- 11.30 a.m.   Post mortem
- 3.00+ p.m.   Collation of campaign intelligence
- 7.00+ p.m.   Preparation of the 'Daily brief'

Conservatives
The Conservatives had the advantage of watching their two main rivals go first. However, it remains significant that, in 1997 at least, the Conservatives were either unwilling or unable to match the extent of Labour's approach to media management.

- 8.30 a.m.   Preparatory meeting
- *9.30 a.m.*   *Daily press conference*
- 8.30 p.m.   Strategy meeting
- 9.00 p.m.   Briefing meeting with John Major

(*Source:* Butler and Kavanagh, 1997)

Box 5.2 Prioritising the news

The importance of the 'running order' of news items is exemplified by the row between Alastair Campbell and BBC producer Kevin Marsh in March 1997 over Marsh's decision to lead with a radio news story about Labour's alleged breach of Commons protocol. For Campbell, however, the real story was John Major's determination to suppress evidence of Tory sleaze prior to a general election. The fact that Marsh had defined the news in a very different way was, to Campbell at least, clear evidence of anti-Labour bias among BBC reporters, something which would continue to shape his attitude to the Corporation in the years which followed.

the broadcasters who determine the headlines and it is these which the press conference seeks to influence.

As we saw in Chapter 2, the communications grid informs the media of the location and activities of each day's campaigning in order that they can be on hand to report. Such events will be organised around the requirements of the teatime and evening news broadcasts, together with the evening editions of the relevant regional and local newspapers. Its dominant feature is the photo opportunity. This is a staged event, which exists to pressure the media into filming and photographing politicians in carefully chosen and advantageous settings. For example, when the message grid lists health care as that day's campaign theme, a hospital or other health care unit has to be found for the leader to visit; where the theme is education, the location will shift to a school or nursery, and so on.

The photo-op seeks to exploit the psychological power of the visual image, in particular its capacity to associate 'an individual or a party . . . [with] certain characteristics or qualities'. This, above all, is why political television is so important. An early master of the photo-op, Lord Bell, has commented to the effect that: 'TV is about imagery – the way it works is by giving impressions. It's hard to get people to listen to words, it's the image that counts.' Unsurprisingly, a young Tony Blair concurred, adding that 'everything' has to be assessed for its visual impact and, by definition, its suitability in the eyes of the TV producers (Rosenbaum 1997: 82–4). The power of

Box 5.3 The decline of the political interview

The influence of the spin doctor has had adverse consequences for the political interview. Whereas the latter was originally constructed around the concept of a dialogue, its modern variant invariably degenerates into a battle between journalist and politician. Its most significant feature is the determination of politicians to communicate their messages regardless of the questions they are asked. Inevitably, interviewers respond by questioning politicians aggressively in order to expose the vacuity of their responses, a development which, in turn, has led media managers to prepare their clients much more thoroughly.

Training
Politicians are schooled in a variety of techniques to 'wrong foot' interviewers, including feigning anger, persistent interruption, insisting a question has been answered already and throwing out the schedule by answering 'questions' before they have been asked.

Restricting access
Politicians who are deemed to be unsatisfactory interviewees are pressurised into refusing requests.

Avoidance
Media managers compile lists of interviewers who are deemed unsuitable. The most famous example of this was Gordon Reece's decision to steer Margaret Thatcher towards 'lighter' programmes, most famously Jimmy Young's late morning show on BBC Radio 2 (the 'JY Prog').

Refusing requests
Where an interviewer or programme is deemed to be 'beyond the pale', media managers can threaten to refuse all future requests for interviews. This tactic was famously deployed in 1997 by Labour party media chief Dave Hill in respect of '**the John Humphrys problem**'.

the photo-op is such that even the most cynical journalists find its allure hard to resist. Professor Kuhn (2007: 244–5) explains why:

While it may well be that some television journalists on the ground have become more sceptical of, and hostile to, their allotted passive role in the parties' staged media events, it can still be difficult for a television reporter to present a piece that goes against the pictures.

The photo-op is the close cousin of the 'sound bite'. As the average time devoted to each news item grew ever smaller, spin doctors realised that they needed to provide editors with a statement so compelling that it would demand inclusion in a way which enabled it to shape the remainder of the news report. The sound bite has a long history. In the 1960s, Harold Wilson would routinely change both the tone and content of his speeches as soon as the TV news cameras were ready to record. However, like so many aspects of party political communication, it came of age with the ascendancy of Margaret Thatcher when her now famous exhortation to the 1980 Conservative party conference – 'You turn if you want to. The lady's not for turning' – captured the spirit of defiance and moral authority which went on to define the next phase of her premiership. Today, they are such a routine feature of political communication that the ability to script them is an essential stock-in-trade of even the most junior press and publicity officer.

Stage management: rallies and the decline of the public meeting

During election campaigns, the photo-op and the sound bite come together in the election rally. This is the ultimate 'pseudo-event' and is unashamedly aimed at 'the millions who see short extracts on television, not . . . the thousands or hundreds actually present' (Rosenbaum 1997: 131). Though the modern rally emerged in the late 1960s, it was the Conservatives' decision to recruit **Harvey Thomas** in 1978 that transformed it into a major media event. Thomas's great skill lay in staging rallies as theatrical productions, with dramatic sets, elaborate lighting rigs and extensive use of stars from sport and show business. He also understood the importance of making the audience part of the performance. By the time Margaret Thatcher arrived on stage, she would be guaranteed a rapturous welcome and the TV news cameras perfect material.

The benefits of this approach were played out to great effect on the Sunday before polling day in 1983, when both Thatcher and her Labour rival Michael Foot addressed rallies in London. Thatcher spoke to 2,500 raucous and often silly Young Conservatives at Wembley, Foot to a much more sizeable gathering which had assembled to welcome the **People's March for Jobs** as it arrived in Hyde Park. The constrast – in terms of size and gravitas – could not have been starker. Yet it was the Conservatives' event that attracted all the media coverage. The reason was quite simple: Thomas's style of rally 'look[s] good on TV. Television loves the movement, the excitement, the star-studded cast-lists' (Rosenbaum 1997: 134).

Inevitably, the Labour party caught on, even though, as at Sheffield in April 1992 (see Box 5.7), it did not always get it right. Inevitably, too, there have been casualties. Political oration is one of these. Similarly, the 'walkabout' and the public meeting have largely disappeared in favour of all-ticket, no-questions events. This does not mean that politicians can completely avoid meeting the public. The party leaders, in particular, are effectively compelled to attend events organised by the broadcasters, in which they have to answer questions from the audience. (In 2005, Labour deliberately exposed Tony Blair to an unusually high number of these, in a manufactured attempt to show the prime minister's humility in the face of persistent accusations of arrogance and abuse of power.) In addition, members of the public will occasionally 'muscle in' uninvited on their photo-ops. No one who saw it will ever forget Tony Blair's acute discomfort when he encountered **Sharon Storrer** outside a Birmingham general hospital in 2001. Indeed, his response – to unsuccessfully usher Ms

---

Box 5.4 Shaping the news cycle

- Enter the news cycle as early as possible.
- Retain momentum by having additional stories (and appropriate 'steers') which enable you to re-enter the cycle as often as possible.
- Ensure that your stories draw the media's attention to the perceived failings of the opposition.
- Finally, always aim to keep one's opponents on the defensive, in order that their own favoured stories are lost as they are continually compelled to defend a weak position.

(*Source:* Gould 1998)

Storrer away from the cameras on the promise (no doubt genuine) of a private audience – was typical of politicians unused to handling reality when it is shouting back at them from three feet away. For the most part, however, such incidents are rare. It is certainly inconceivable that a leading politician will be filmed being browbeaten by a hostile public meeting in the manner of Alec Douglas-Home during the 1964 general election.

Spinning

These and other techniques have given media managers unprecedented influence over the coverage of election campaigns. However, they are only too aware that things still can and do go horribly wrong. There are numerous and complex reasons for this, wrapped up in the changing technology and culture of the media. As a result, even the most professional operation is vulnerable to the unexpected. A leaked document, an unscripted comment, embarrassing research findings – each has the short-term capacity to throw into chaos the communications grid and, in the long term, to 'frame' (see Chapter 7) media reports about a party *per se*. For example, in 1992 hostile reporting over Neil Kinnock's suitability as a prime minister, allied to Labour's inability to rebut Conservative propaganda over its fiscal policy, ensured that Labour failed to shift media attention to its preferred agenda of 'caring' issues such as health care. Even when the latter did capture the news headlines, coverage focused on the morality of Labour's decision to use real cases of alleged medical failings for its propaganda rather than the state of the nation's hospitals (Kuhn 2007: 247).

This no doubt helps explain why New Labour subsequently set the standard for 'spinning' news stories. Their approach has been summarised by a former government information officer as the three 'Rs': rhetoric, repetition and rebuttal (Franklin 2004: 69). The first demands absolute consistency in the delivery of key messages; the second, constant repetition; and the third, immediate and robust responses to hostile stories. Sometimes a spin doctor will deploy more subtle techniques to this effect (see Box 5.5). More often than not, however, these are secondary to much more aggressive forms of treatment (Franklin 2004: 29), via which Alastair Campbell, in particular, acquired his reputation for cheerful brutality. The results can be seen in the following list:

- Spin doctors are vociferous complainers. Broadcasters are particularly vulnerable since they are obliged to be impartial as a result of the regulatory framework under which they operate.
- Their complaints are often highly personal. New Labour's media managers in particular encouraged the view that they maintained a dossier on political journalists, via which their loyalty, influence and so on could be monitored and evaluated. Even those, such as George Jones of the *Daily Telegraph* and David Hencke of *The Guardian*, who wished to cooperate but who worked for editors who did not, were marginalised.
- More disturbingly, attacks extend to what Oborne and Walters (2004: 201) call the destabilisation of individual journalists in the eyes of their employers. Franklin (2004: 30) cites Campbell's lobbying of David Montgomery (CEO of *The Independent*) prior to the dismissal of Andrew Marr as one among numerous examples.

Monitoring and rebuttal

Spinning depends upon the ability to respond immediately whenever adverse changes to the news cycle threaten. This has given rise to the widespread use of media monitoring and rebuttal. Like so many aspects of party political communication, this technique was imported from the US. In 1988 the Democrat party's presidential campaign was derailed in the face of a sustained media assault, inspired and in part directed by the Republican party machine. With so much smear and innuendo circulating in the political ether, Democrat campaign managers found it impossible to refocus the attention of journalists onto their chosen stories. As a result, their candidate, Michael Dukakis, was permanently on the defensive, trying forlornly to press ahead with attacks on his Republican rival via a media which was not listening to him. As noted above, four years later the Labour party's general election campaign underwent a similar crisis. Its failure to respond effectively in summer 1991 when the Conservatives first launched their long campaign made it impossible to move the media

Box 5.5 Alastair Campbell and the 'dark arts'

Exclusives
Campbell routinely used 'exclusives' to reward favoured journalists. Among the first to receive his attentions were Tony Bevins (*Independent*) and Philip Webster (*The Times*); later Patrick Wintour (*Guardian*) and Tom Baldwin (also of *The Times*) were added to this group. However, the principal beneficiary of Campbell's largesse was *The Sun*. The list of 'scoops' sent its way most famously includes President Clinton's written appeal for peace in Northern Ireland, Cherie Blair's pregnancy and the date of the 2001 general election.

Providing copy
Campbell famously wrote hundreds of articles which went out under Blair's name; so many in fact that Blair once received a rather tongue-in-cheek award for his contribution to journalism. Once again, the principal beneficiaries were those papers like *The Sun* whose readers Blair and Campbell most wished to influence.

Steering
Steering works by encouraging journalists to cover a particular story at the expense of others. This includes *firebreaking*, whereby journalists are diverted from a potentially embarrassing story. Sometimes steers are false, winning favourable publicity at the expense of long-term credibility. One particularly notorious example of this was the revelation that Blair was about to launch a new, authoritarian initiative on social security in January 1999 when no such thing was ever planned or delivered.

Pre-empting
This minimises the impact of embarrassing revelations by announcing them publicly before they are published or broadcast. This is closely associated with *pre-buttal*, when opposition criticisms are rubbished before they have been made.

Concealment
This is a particularly notorious technique, which times the release of damaging information so that it is unlikely to be taken up by the media. Thanks in particular to Jo Moore's ill-starred intervention at the time of 9/11, it will be forever associated with New Labour as a mark of its cynicism and disregard for the public interest.

Outright denials

Ultimately, however, spin doctors will deny outright stories which appear to have contained an element of truth. Perhaps the most notorious example of this was Campbell's denial that Blair had intervened on behalf of Rupert Murdoch as he attempted to purchase the Italian broadcaster Mediaset for £4 billion in April 1998. Campbell's defence was based on his interpretation of the word 'intervention'. Apparently, Blair had not intervened because he had not instigated the conversation with Italian prime minister, Romano Prodi. Another technique used by Campbell to this effect was to seize upon a minor factual error and use it in an attempt to undermine the entire story, an example being the manner in which he dealt with Matthew Parris's account of Euan Blair's entry to the London Oratory school.

agenda on from tax and spending when the official campaign began in earnest eight months or so later.

Little Rock

However, back in the US the Democrats had learned the lessons from their defeat. Philip Gould (see the glossary at the end of chapter 1) recounts how the Clinton campaign team in Little Rock, Arkansas, prepared for the all-important first televised debate between their candidate and the Republican incumbent, George Bush. This provides a classic example of how monitoring and rebuttal should work. Prior to the debate, Democrat campaigners had researched what Gould describes as 12 thick volumes of articles, factual summaries and other documents which focused on both Bush's perceived weaknesses and, more importantly, the likely lines of Republican attack. During the debate, Democrat officials identified each and every one of Bush's criticisms of Clinton, cross-referenced these against the volumes of rebuttal, prepared counter-arguments and transmitted these electronically to over 200 media organisations, and all before the broadcast had ended.

The Democrats' approach recognised that the failure to immediately rebut damaging arguments can prove ruinous. Regardless of their accuracy, they can be taken up by the media and enter the public domain as unchallenged fact. This had unhinged the Dukakis campaign and Clinton's principal campaign managers were determined not to let it happen again.

The world of politics is littered with assertions that are untrue, but are believed to be true because they were not effectively answered. An unrebutted lie becomes accepted as the truth. You must always rebut a political attack if leaving it unanswered will harm you. And you must do it instantly. (Gould 1998: 295)

Monitoring and rebuttal in the 1997 general election
Gould had little difficulty in selling monitoring and rebuttal to Tony Blair two years later. The importance Labour's high command attached to it was such that when Peter Mandelson took over Labour's campaign headquarters in March 1996, it was accorded top priority. Labour also purchased the Excalibur computer system to assemble rebuttal arguments on an electronic database. The particular value of Excalibur was that it could scan instantaneously all manner of documents like a photocopier. However, it is indicative of the speed with which a war room geared towards rapid rebuttal can work that many of Labour's campaign staff preferred to use their hard copy in order to maximise the speed of their response. The benefits to the Labour party were numerous:

- Firstly, and unlike the situation five years previously, the Conservatives' first major attack on tax in November 1996 was convincingly rebutted within three hours. According to Gould (1998: 166) this had such a dispiriting effect on the Conservatives that tax was largely killed off as election issue.
- Secondly, it enabled Labour to give the media stories which continually put the spotlight on their opponents' perceived shortcomings, thereby denying them the opportunity to campaign on their preferred issues or themes.
- Thirdly, Labour was able to concentrate its fire on journalists themselves. Thanks to its database, Labour's complaints about media bias 'were inevitably well researched and sensibly focused' (Oborne and Walters 2004: 125). As a result, producers and editors who might otherwise have been minded to dismiss them found it much harder to do so.
- Fourthly, monitoring helped keep candidates 'on message' by alerting them to the latest campaign developments, potentially difficult questions and how best to respond to them. This reduced the

possibility that a candidate might answer in a way which hinted at uncertainty or disagreement and acted to preserve the integrity of the campaign grid.

- Less positively, campaign managers could much more easily monitor the comments of those candidates known to go 'off message' and bar them from accepting further interview requests (Oborne and Walters 2004: 124–5). These authors quote the examples of Clare Short and Austin Mitchell who were contacted within minutes of making unfavourable comments and ordered not to conduct further interviews.

Of course, applying this degree of pressure on MPs who have well-deserved reputations for independence of thought and action is much easier when a party is seeking power after nearly two decades in opposition. It becomes much harder to apply when the thirst for power has been slaked somewhat and when the authority of the party leadership has been diminished by events. This was certainly the experience of Blair and Campbell after 2001, who were unable to exert quite the same degree of control from this point.

Image management

Media management has had important consequences for the use (and abuse) of personal image. This was so as early as the 1920s when the advent of the newsreel first compelled politicians to consider how their physical appearances might play before cinema audiences. Fast forward eight decades and we enter a world where media managers now aim to construct complete public personas for their clients in ways calculated to maximise their political appeal.

How they attempt to do this is set out in Box 5.6. They tell us that, whilst a politician's beliefs and conduct are important, image-making is also shaped by a range of factors which have little obvious connection with politics. Indeed, this type of image management stems from the fact that few voters ever meet politicians. Consequently, media representations of them play the dominant role in shaping public perceptions. Televisual images are particularly important because human beings tend automatically to associate appearance with personality. We are all vulnerable to powerful cultural stereotypes which

Box 5.6 Image manufacture

Physical qualities
Politicians may attempt to modify these to make themselves more acceptable to voters. Margaret Thatcher did so successfully with the pitch and timbre of her voice; Alec Douglas-Home less so with his rather cadaverous visage.

Grooming
The examples of politicians altering clothing and hairstyle to strike a better impression are too numerous to list. Whilst Margaret Thatcher undoubtedly set new standards in this respect, grooming is by no means confined to women. John Major, for instance, was rumoured to be notoriously fussy in his preparations before appearing on camera.

Props
Though perhaps not as prominent today as they once were, politicians will use props to convey particular messages. For example, Churchill's Havana cigars spoke of power and authority and duly met their counterpart in the integrity and dependability conveyed through Clement Attlee's pipe. One of Attlee's successors, Harold Wilson, also used a pipe (for identical purposes) even when he, like Churchill, was a regular cigar smoker.

Families
Beginning with (the unmarried) Edward Heath's career as Conservative leader (1965–75), campaign advisers have become obsessed about the need for family support. On occasion, the public image of a leader's spouse has been deployed as an election asset, as was the case with Norma Major in 1992. Voters' perceptions of her as the likeable-woman-next-door perfectly complemented the image her husband was trying to develop and contrasted strongly with that of Glennis Kinnock whose career as a high-profile politician in her own right was not believed to play well with 'Middle England'.

Interests and personal histories
This is perhaps the most interesting area of all, not least because it has led politicians to go through some interesting chronological contortions. Neil Kinnock offered a case in point when he placed particular emphasis on the fact that he was the first Kinnock for 'a thousand generations' (that is, 3,000 years) to go to university. More

famously, Tony Blair found himself in a spot of media bother after making claims that he had, as a boy, tried to stow away in an aircraft and delighted in watching Newcastle and England legend Jackie Milburn play football at St James' Park. The first was, according to his father, most unlikely; the second, quite impossible.

Incumbency
This is an advantage enjoyed by the prime minister. Providing it is properly planned and timed, high-level summitry in particular is a very obvious way of emphasising the PM's statesmanship to the detriment of the leaders of the opposition parties.

shape our ideas about how certain people, including political leaders, should look. This appearance–personality nexus, of course, may be completely deceptive. However, this will not necessarily diminish its impact. Unless they possess unusual degrees of political insight, most voters' views on politicians' 'competence, compassion, likeability, authority, sincerity and strength of purpose' will be made 'partly on the basis of how they look' (Rosenbaum 1997: 180).

Yet, personal image is only partly a function of physical appearance. For example, as British society became less deferential in the 1960s, being seen as a 'man (or woman) of the people' has become a required feature of image construction. This development owes much to Harold Wilson who famously likened his preferred image to that of a family doctor: professional, dependable and trustworthy. It also helps explain why male political leaders choose to make so much of their interest in sport (even to a point of rewriting their personal histories).

Political images
However, perhaps the most interesting aspect of image management is its impact on the ways in which parties conduct their internal business. This is an umbrella term that covers policy-making, internal elections and candidate selection. For media managers, each of these is a political 'minefield', essentially because the media are naturally drawn to any signs of internal dissent and challenges to the leader's authority. No party is immune and such is the near-obsession with projecting a collective image of unity under the party leadership that spin doctors

Box 5.7 When it all goes wrong: the case of Neil Kinnock

Neil Kinnock presents us with something of a conundrum. A moderniser who was very aware of the importance of professional communications, it is highly ironic that his campaigning was blighted by a series of PR 'gaffes' which occurred precisely because he followed the advice of his media managers. The first of these happened in 1987. Trying desperately to demonstrate his statesmanlike qualities, he sought an audience with US President Ronald Reagan, a known admirer of his bitter rival Margaret Thatcher. The result was a disaster, not least because Reagan at first feigned not to recognise him as the Leader of the Opposition. Five years later, he blundered again, this time by getting highly emotional at the infamous Sheffield rally, where, much to the dismay of his campaign team, he bounded on to the stage repeatedly shouting 'We're all right!'.

invariably react with increasing hostility to the first sign of disloyalty, even when the latter results from accident rather than design.

In the 2005 general election, a particularly dramatic example of this was Michael Howard's response to Howard Flight's speech, secretly recorded and then released to the media, which stated that Conservative spending cuts would be far greater in government than they had promised in opposition. This was a particularly sensitive issue for Howard. Not content with the fact that Flight immediately resigned as deputy chairman of the Conservative party, Howard withdrew the party whip, effectively sacking him as MP for Arundel and South Downs. A major row then broke out, not least because Flight's constituency association insisted that they should decide who their candidate should be. Though a deal was eventually patched together, the affair illustrated the remarkable sensitivity that exists towards ill-discipline in a media-dominated age.

In the Labour party, however, this trend reached such a point that its internal constitution has been completely overhauled (see Box 5.8). This process began under Neil Kinnock (Foster 1994) and continued under the leaderships of both John Smith and especially Tony Blair. In essence, it is part of an ongoing reaction to Labour's experience of government in the 1970s, which as Lewis Baston (2001: 163) notes was wholly debilitating:

Box 5.8 Reforming the party: Labour under Tony Blair

National Executive Committee (NEC)
Reforms in 1997 changed the composition of the NEC in the leadership's favour, thereby making it impossible for high-profile left-wing MPs to use it an alternative power base.

The annual party conference
This was also brought under leadership control, principally by downgrading its policy-making function in favour of a new National Policy Forum (NPF) and a joint policy committee dominated by Cabinet ministers. Party managers were also determined to impose greater discipline on individual delegates, something which dramatically backfired in the case of **Walter Wolfgang**.

Candidate selection
In addition to a series of rule-changes, most notably in the selection of Labour's would-be MEPs and MSPs, the party leadership routinely engaged in high-profile lobbying to secure the selection of its preferred candidates.

Bypassing activists
Running through all of these internal reforms was a belief that the constitution gave too much power to party activists at the expense of individual members. The creation of the NPF, the use of ballots to rewrite Clause IV and ratify the 1997 party manifesto and the tentative attempt to restructure constituency parties all bear witness to Blair's determination to change the character and culture of his party.

The poor state of relations between party and government . . . had a bad effect. It presented an unattractive picture of a divided party and . . . attracted accusations that Labour was becoming extreme. It also handicapped the party's organizational ability to present its case at general elections.

Concern over an adverse media reaction is only one of a number of explanatory factors. However, it is significant that levels of internal dissent which might have been tolerated in the 1960s and 70s were suppressed as soon as the party began to modernise its political communications after 1985. Regrettably, there is not the available space to do much more than 'flag' this connection in this particular study. However, the reader is urged to bear in mind the fact that a decision to push party propaganda to voters indirectly via the media can have implications both for the conduct of public life and for our very understanding of democratic practice.

Conclusion

In this chapter we have examined the concept of news management and the pivotal role it continues to play in party political communications. Indeed, so intensive has the battle for control of the day's news agenda become that it has forced its way beyond election campaigning and into day-to-day politics. One consequence of this has been the manner in which government, too, has been drawn into daily news management to a degree which is quite unparalleled in peace time. The importance of this development cannot be overstated. In contrast to the opposition parties, the government is in a uniquely powerful position to control media content. The extent of its power and the implications this has had for the conduct of politics will be the subject of the next chapter.

. . . .

What you should have learnt from reading this chapter

- The ways in which parties organise their electoral campaigning for the benefit of the media.
- How the photo-op, sound bite and party rally have evolved to help secure favourable media coverage.
- Why spin doctors have emerged as such key players in party political communications and why they place so much emphasis on monitoring and rebuttal.
- The several ways in which media and image management have impacted upon party organisation, discipline and policy-making.

Glossary of key terms

People's March for Jobs This was organised by trade unions to protest against the economic policies of the Thatcher government, which they blamed for a dramatic rise in unemployment. The march consisted originally of unemployed workers, who set out from Glasgow and arrived in London just before the 1983 general election.

Sharon Storrer Briefly, Ms Storrer became a media sensation after she confronted Tony Blair outside a Birmingham hospital on the day Labour launched its manifesto for the 2001 general election. She was incensed by the medical treatment received by her husband – a cancer patient – and left the prime minister in no doubt about the inadequacy of Labour's management of the NHS.

The John Humphrys problem This was the description used by the Labour party director of communications, Dave Hill, to describe his frustration at the manner in which revered BBC radio presenter John Humphrys had questioned Secretary of State for Social Security Harriet Harman in a radio interview in 1997. More generally, it captures spin doctors' intense dislike of aggressive broadcast interviewers following in the tradition of the late Sir Robin Day.

Harvey Thomas Thomas served as press and public relations director to Margaret Thatcher during her time as prime minister. He had acquired remarkable insight into event management whilst working for TV evangelist Billy Graham and brought this to bear on Conservative PR throughout the late 1970s and 1980s.

Walter Wolfgang Born in Germany of Jewish parents in 1923, Wolfgang and his family fled to the UK when he was 14 to escape Nazi persecution. He joined the Labour party in 1948 and stood unsuccessfully for parliament in the 1959 general election. After a lifetime of low-profile political activism, Wolfgang suddenly became a media figure when, aged 82, he was forcibly ejected from the 2005 Labour party conference for shouting 'Nonsense' during a speech being delivered by Jack Straw. The fact that Wolfgang was later held under s. 44 of the Terrorism Act 2000 seemed only to confirm the accusations of intolerance and authoritarianism widely leveled at New Labour. On the back of his new-found prominence, Wolfgang was elected to Labour's National Executive Committee in 2006.

Likely examination questions

What factors explain the prominence of the spin doctor in modern political communications?

In what ways do political parties seek to manage the media?

What are the implications of media management techniques for internal party democracy?

Helpful websites

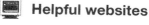

The campaigning group Spinwatch is dedicated to monitoring PR activities across the corporate world has a very interesting, campaign-orientated website, which can be found at www.spinwatch.com. Leading BBC journalist and veteran 'spin decoder' Nicholas Jones has his own site at www.nicholasjones.org.uk which is very much worth a visit.

 Further reading

An excellent and wide-ranging history of both media and image management can be found in Chapters 4 to 5 and 7 to 8 of Rosenbaum's *From Soapbox to Soundbite*. Chapter 7 of McNair's *Introduction to Political Communication* provides a very useful overview of contemporary developments, whilst Bob Franklin devotes the second chapter of *Packaging Politics* to an analysis of New Labour's record on spin. Peter Oborne and Simon Walters' 2004 *Alastair Campbell* (London: Aurum) is a hugely entertaining if partisan account of the most celebrated spin doctor of the modern era, whilst Nicholas Jones's 1996 *Soundbites and Spin Doctors* (London: Cassell) is an excellent overview of the rise of the spin doctor, albeit from the perspective of a leading journalist.

Government Communications

Contents

Overview

Despite accusations that they routinely overlooked political communications, governments in the UK have steadily acquired a powerful capacity to control the ebb and flow of official information. After 1997, however, this trend was accelerated to a degree which was quite unprecedented. Controversy followed hard on its heels and, in so many ways, continues to define the Blair–Brown era. This chapter will seek to explain the changes put in place during this period and why Labour's plans for media management went so badly wrong.

Key issues to be covered in this chapter

- The evolution of government communications during the twentieth century
- The reforms initiated by the Blair government
- The events surrounding the resignation of Alastair Campbell as Director of Communications in August 2003
- The implications of the emergence of a public relations state

The government's media machine

Two tensions run through government communications. Firstly, ministers have to balance the historic pressures to keep their conduct hidden from view with the need to continually shape the news agenda. Secondly, whether the government is aiming to push news into the media domain or keep it secret, it has to decide how best this might be done: covertly, via interpersonal contacts, or overtly through methods such as high-profile criminal prosecutions. The main options at its disposal are set out below:

- Overt concealment via censorship
- Covert concealment through high-level political contacts
- Overt release through the official agencies now grouped into the Government Communications Network (GCN) and
- Covert release through semi-official mechanisms such as the lobby system.

This section will explore each in turn.

Censorship

This is dominated by the law on official secrecy (1911–89), which has consistently asserted ministers' status as the sole legitimate arbiters of the decision to release official information. According to the view within Whitehall, this status – which is wrapped up in ministers' duty to protect the national interest – overrides all other considerations, including the duty of the media to report.

Official secrecy law enables ministers to prevent the broadcast or publication of journalistic material through court injunctions. In addition, it also allows government law officers to bring criminal prosecutions against both journalists and the so-called 'whistle-blowers' who supply them with their information. Today journalists are most likely to be prosecuted under the 1989 Act, which protects official secrecy in four specific areas: security and intelligence; defence; international affairs; and information that leads to the commission of criminal offences or which compromises the efficiency of the criminal justice system. Convictions under these provisions will typically carry a maximum custodial sentence of two years.

Box 6.1 Selected offences under the Official Secrets Act

The 1911 Official Secrets Act

- Under s. 1(b) it is an offence to make a note which is either calculated or might be useful to an enemy.

The 1989 Official Secrets Act

- Under s. 1 it is an offence for the media to publish any disclosures from existing or former members of the security or intelligence services relating to their work.
- Under s. 5 the media must not publish information known to be protected by the Act, where publication is and is known to be damaging to UK interests.
- Under s. 6 it is an offence to disclose information that originally came from another state or an international organisation.
- Journalists commit an offence under s. 8 if they possess documents or articles containing information falling into one of three categories: items disclosed by a government employee; items trusted to someone in confidence by a government employee; or items entrusted in confidence to other states or international organisations.

Official secrecy legislation is complemented by a second body of law (see Box 6.2) which compels journalists to reveal both their sources and source material. Further, these offences grant police officers extensive search and seizure powers. Journalists have particular reason to be mindful of s. 9 of the Official Secrets Act 1911, a very wide-ranging provision which enables the police to forcibly enter their homes and offices to search for and seize any material which is evidence of any offence under the Act.

Whilst it is rare for journalists to be prosecuted, the law has been used to pressurise those who subject government conduct to unusually high degrees of criticism. Perhaps the most infamous example of this was the February 1987 special branch raid on the offices of BBC Scotland during the Zircon spy satellite affair, a raid described by the then assistant director general of the BBC as 'a shabby, shameful, disgraceful state-sponsored incursion'.

Box 6.2 The law on compulsory disclosure of sources and source material

Contempt of Court Act 1981
The authorities can seek court orders demanding journalists reveal their sources in the interests of security or justice, or for the prevention of crime and disorder. A failure to obey exposes them to a prison sentence for contempt of court.

Police and Criminal Evidence Act 1984
This enables police officers to secure the support of journalists as witnesses or suppliers of information. Whilst journalists cannot be compelled to answer police questions, they can be ordered to hand over information.

The Official Secrets Acts 1920 and 1939
Under s. 6 of the 1920 Act (as amended in 1939) a senior police officer can compel a journalist to disclose any information about alleged espionage. Failure to comply is a criminal offence.

Terrorism Act 2000
Under s. 19 a journalist who withholds information which suggests that a person is involved in financing terrorism commits an offence. More wide ranging still is s. 38B, which makes it a criminal offence to withhold any information of suspected terrorism offences and offers journalists no special protection. S. 39 criminalises the disclosure or publication of any information which is likely to prejudice a terrorist investigation, whilst s. 58 makes it any offence to collect, record or possess information which is likely to be of use in the preparation or commission of a terrorist offence. A journalist's notes would obviously fall into this category.

Financial and organisational levers

These offer a covert alternative to censorship. They work by exploiting the media's political dependence upon government.

- The very structure of the media and the regulatory system under which it operates can be radically changed by parliamentary legislation.
- More specifically, the BBC relies on ministers both for its Charter and its licence fee. Most recently, former director general Greg

Dyke has argued that the Blair government deliberately under-funded the BBC in order to create a culture of dependency within the Corporation (Franklin 2004: 356).

- Government control over broadcasting is further enhanced by its powers of patronage, most obviously of the BBC Board of Governors (now the BBC Trust) and the chairman and other key members of Ofcom.

The use of patronage is particularly controversial. Margaret Thatcher (though she is by no means alone in this) was accused of 'packing' the BBC Board of Governors with political favourites, whom she later used to influence BBC programme content. This was most notably so in 1985, when Leon Brittan pressurised the BBC Board of Governors into postponing and then re-editing the infamous *Real Lives* programme on terrorism in Northern Ireland. According to Franklin (2004: 30), the long-term effect of such intimi-dation 'has been to undermine journalists' self-confidence, encour-age self-censorship and create a climate which is typically hostile to investigative journalism'.

The Central Office of Information (CIO) and the Government Information and Communications System (GICS)

The CIO and GICS offer ministers a different set of options, their role being to facilitate the release of official information into the public domain. The CIO was formed after World War II as the principal agency of government publicity. Following extensive reor-ganisation during the Thatcher years, its role changed to one of budgetary management and coordination. However, this has not prevented an exponential expansion in its budget, leading (as we saw in Chapter 4) to widespread criticism that the governing party uses the CIO to supplement its private political advertising. Such allega-tions were made with particular vehemence in the run up to the 2001 general election.

By contrast, the GICS is tasked with explaining departmental policy to the media and beyond. It consists of an interdepartmental network of 1,200 or so information officers and other media spe-cialists, their 300 regional counterparts in the Government News

Table 6.1 CIO expenditure			
	Staffing	Costs (£m)	Expenditure (£m)
1983–4	not available	22	60.5
1987–8	804	18	141
1997–8	not available	16.6	125.9
2000–1	399	20.8	295.4

(*Source:* Franklin 2004: 77)

Network and the staff based in 10 Downing Street itself. Historically their job has been to issue press statements and other news items for media consumption. Once again, however, changes during the Thatcher years brought centralising pressures to bear which ensured that their work became integrated much more closely with that of the prime minister's press office. In the process the prime minister's chief press secretary became the de facto and later the formal head of the departmental information officers.

Managing the lobby

The chief press secretary – a post which dates from 1929 – also plays the key role in the fourth and in so many respects the most important of the main mechanisms of government communication: managing the lobby. This is the collective term for the 220 or so accredited journalists, drawn from television, radio and the newspapers, who attend the twice-daily briefings given on the prime minister's behalf. Led de facto by the most senior political editors of the day, the lobby is the key source of political news in both the broadcast and print media (Franklin 2004: 43). There are three reasons for this:

- Firstly, there is a structured regularity to their meetings.
- Secondly, lobby journalists appreciate that they are being briefed by a person who can speak authoritatively on behalf of the prime minister.
- Thirdly, by cooperating with the prime minister they stand a good chance of picking up a wide range of highly newsworthy 'steers'

and 'titbits', not least about the *faux pas* (real and imagined) of the prime minister's internal political rivals.

In these circumstances, the great manipulators of the lobby can earn for the government a huge advantage in the daily battle for control of the news agenda. Almost inevitably, however, the main beneficiaries have been the '[s]uccessive prime ministers [who] discovered that an effective press secretary could play a vital role in imposing their own version of events on Whitehall' (Oborne and Walters 2004: 146). More than any other institution, the lobby reminds us of the media's dependence on the government as 'its greatest single source of information' (Whale 1980: 117). The news media in particular could not exist in its current form unless ministers, their officials and leading members of the governing party supplied them with the necessary information and interview opportunities they require. This is even truer today when the changing internal economics of news production have placed an ever greater emphasis on low-cost journalism, or 'churnalism' (Davies 2006).

'Millbankisation' and 'Washingtonisation': the transformation of government communications after 1997

However, the government's already formidable media armoury was not enough to satisfy the hugely ambitious media management strategy New Labour intended to deploy in office. As Bartle (2006: 126) notes:

> The relationship between the Labour government and the media has simultaneously been more continuous, more intense and more fraught than any other in British history. Indeed, for some critics, an obsessive concern with presentation, spin and controlling its press is the defining characterisitic of New Labour.

All governments worry about communications, not least because of the fear that ministers will become enamoured of their new-found status and use it to develop their own private political agendas. However, in New Labour's case a host of additional factors also shaped government policy:

- Despite his 179-seat majority, Tony Blair had few illusions about his party's electoral popularity or, indeed, the loyalty of leading newspapers.
- Labour's communications strategy had been built around Blair himself and aimed 'to convey through the media an image of leadership which is consonant with public expectations about how a leader should perform' (Lees-Marshment 2001: 146). As a result the new government was under additional pressure to keep out of the media spotlight those MPs and ministers whose loyalty to the new prime minister and his '**project**' was anything but certain.
- New Labour's decision to abandon positional politics effectively meant that voters' evaluation of its first term would hinge on the facts of its record in office. This demanded a daily barrage of government information and rebuttal, together with a battle with journalists to ensure that the government's view received 'top billing'.

However, there is also strong evidence that a degree of fear and loathing influenced New Labour's response. This dated from the Kinnock era: the formative period for the Blair leadership. Consequently, the party's attitude to the media was highly ambiguous. Whilst it respected the media's power, it was also deeply cynical towards political journalists, the latter being memorably described by Campbell as 'the disillusionment industry' (Scammell 2001: 514).

Managing ministers

The first element of Labour's reforms – 'Millbankisation' – refers to the transplanting of the techniques New Labour had used in its successful 1997 general election campaign. During his very first Cabinet meeting and again on subsequent occasions throughout May, June and July, Blair pointed out to his ministers that he would not tolerate them privately briefing journalists and, further, that Campbell and his staff would be monitoring the media for evidence of this. Finally, and just in case the position had not been made fully clear, the rules of procedure for ministers were subsequently amended in three respects.

- All major interviews and media appearances had to be cleared with Campbell and his staff at the Downing Street press office.

- The content of all major speeches, statements and other policy initiatives had to be sent to the prime minister's private office to be checked prior to release.
- Finally, the timing and form of announcements coming from departments had to be authorised by the press office to ensure they could be fitted properly into the government's communications 'grid'.

Structural changes: the Mountfield Report and after

The attempt to impose greater discipline across government was reinforced by a series of structural reforms. Four months after taking office, the government commissioned Sir Robin Mountfield (then permanent secretary at the Office of Public Service) to report into the GICS's capacity to implement its communications strategy. Margaret Scammell (2001: 523) describes his report as 'as a landmark in the modern history of government presentation' and 'a victory for Labour's brand of news management'. Understandably, Campbell saw the report as giving him the necessary political cover to build a new institutional structure at the heart of government (see Box 6.3).

The keystone of the new arrangements was the Strategic Communications Unit, which used information gathering and planning software to plot government communications against major forthcoming events, including those which had nothing directly to do with the government itself. Each week, Campbell and his team used this information to plan the following week's communications. A draft was presented each Thursday to the various information heads, who were expected to use it to plan their own department's public relations. However, and in addition, Campbell established a team of leading officials from across government which met each morning. Its job was to assess the need for daily adjustments to that week's grid, clarify the government's position and ensure that Campbell was properly prepared for his first meeting with the lobby, at 11.00 a.m.

The parallels between this process and the pre-election planning discussed in Chapter 2 will be obvious.

- Campbell could establish and impose a daily campaign theme across government.
- Unhelpful clashes could be avoided.

Box 6.3 A strategic capacity: strengthening the centre, December 1997 to March 1999

Strategic Communications Unit (SCU)
Created in January 1998, the SCU's main role was to provide the background intelligence on which the government's communications grid is constructed. SCU staff – which numbered six by 2000 – also supported departmental information officers.

The Research and Information Unit (RIU)
This was created in March 1999 as the government's rebuttal service. Its main tasks were to assist the chief press secretary and the SCU by establishing the government's 'line' on key issues, providing key facts, information and quotes in support of government policy, and identifying the impact of government policy in particular regions and constituencies. The RIU used the *Knowledge Network* database which 'replicates in more powerful form the Excalibur computer database used at Millbank in Labour's election campaign' (Scammell 2001: 525).

Media Management Unit
Based in the Cabinet Office, the Media Management Unit was established in December 1997 to ensure that the SCU and all those involved in government communications have the latest information about the daily news agenda.

- Bad news could be released at a time when it neither overshadowed the good nor captured the news headlines. (This was the context in which Jo Moore famously urged the Department of Transport 'to bury bad news' as the World Trade Center crashed to the floor and, later, as the corpse of Princess Margaret awaited interment.)
- All departments could be reminded constantly of the importance of communications and the particular needs of Downing Street.
- In this way, the prime minister could be more easily associated with strategically important and popular policies and distanced from those which were either irrelevant or potentially harmful.
- Most importantly, however, by strengthening its strategic capability, the government was in a much better position to control the

news cycle. If a threatening story emerged, Campbell would know immediately what options he had to counter it. Better still, he would be able to act quickly.

'Washingtonisation': reforming the GICS

The third element of Labour's communications strategy was to change the mindset of government information officers. Mountfield had acknowledged that the GICS was not in a position to implement the government's strategy or to provide ministers with the media services they required and which they had come to expect when in opposition. Part of the problem was constitutional. Like all civil servants, information officers were mindful of their neutrality and the importance of following the procedures which had been laid down to preserve this status. In addition, however, strong cultural factors were also at work. GICS staff were used to standing above the political fray. Though no doubt affronted when their minister received a particularly bad press, they were simply unused to seeing the media as an adversary to be vanquished in a series of running battles. This, of course, was not how Campbell viewed matters.

Relations were complicated further by the constitutional position of the chief press secretary. Whilst it was accepted that the latter could issue instructions, this was always on the assumption that he was, like the rest of the GICS, an orthodox civil servant. This, for example, had made Bernard Ingham's promotion to head of the GIS perfectly proper. Campbell's appointment, however, changed everything. Despite having the title Chief Press Secretary, Campbell was employed as a special adviser and so could not issue orders to GIS staff.

Blair's solution was to issue an order-in-council which gave Campbell a unique constitutional status. Whilst remaining a special adviser, he was also given unprecedented power to issue instructions to information officers. Appropriately armed, Campbell immediately set about remoulding the GICS in his own image. On 5 May 1997, he met the information heads for the first time to inform them of his intention to deploy in government the same media management techniques Labour had used in opposition. His meaning was clear: from this point on, the GICS was to assist him in ensuring that the media published the stories ministers wanted. Campbell amplified his plans in a letter dated 26 September 2007.

- The presentation of policy was critical: consequently, information officers could expect to be thoroughly involved in the policy-making process from the outset.
- Pro-action would be the order of the day: stories had to be given their proper 'build up' if they were to enter the news cycle at the appropriate moment.
- The battle for the news headlines had to be fought and re-fought on a daily basis: like spin doctors, information officers would have to challenge journalists and editors over their choice of headlines.
- The national 'Sundays' in particular should be targeted: where possible, GICS staff would assist them with the development of their stories.
- Official information was not a public resource but a weapon in a political battle: GICS staff needed to understand that the government would release information in order to maximise its political benefits.

Campbell's reasoning is rooted deeply in his (and Blair's) understanding of media bias. However, its net effect was to alter the character and purpose of government communication. This was something which many information officers simply could not countenance. Within a year, 25 of the 44 most senior officials within the GICS were no longer in post, most notably Jill Rutter at the Treasury who publicly complained that most of her role had been taken over by Brown's special adviser, Charlie Whelan. Four years later and the exodus was complete, with all 44 positions in the hands of others. The fact that most of them had been replaced by outsiders – politically acceptable temporary bureaucrats, in the words of Professor Franklin – only compounded speculation that the professionals had been forced from their posts.

This is the background to **Andy Wood**'s use of the term 'Washingtonisation': the idea that a new government will bring with it into office its own staff who will have a personal as well as a professional interest in the administration's political success. The arrival of 'temporary bureaucrats' was only one element of this process. The other was the unprecedented growth in the number of special media advisers across Whitehall. By 2002, a total of 81 special advisers were employed across government, around half of whom worked in media management. However, the popular interest in the cost to the taxpayer – whilst undoubtedly important – rather misses the point. The significance of the special advisers lay not in their numbers but their function. Though some like Whelan could go 'off message', the vast majority of special advisers understood what it was they were there to do. In purely functional terms, this meant checking all departmental press releases to ensure that they met with Campbell's criteria, ensuring that departmental communications dovetailed with the grid established by Campbell and the SCU and, most importantly, taking the fight to the media as they might do during an election campaign. For a while, these new arrangements swept all before them. As events were soon to demonstrate, however, whatever early successes 'Millbankisation' and 'Washingtonisation' might have delivered, they were soon to prove Labour's and particularly Campbell's undoing.

After hubris, nemesis

New Labour arrived in Whitehall with a swagger, a mission and a very obvious sense of historic grievance. For a while, the media seemed enthralled by the new government and largely reported the conduct of New Labour ministers very much as the latter would have wanted. With hindsight, however, it was inevitable that this extended 'honeymoon' would end at some point. By 1999, editors had duly concluded that the election of the first Labour government for 23 years was no longer the story and that their journalists must look elsewhere for 'news'. It was a change in response which seemed to take the government unawares.

For those with the eyes to see, there had been early signs of disaffection, notably the media's response to allegations of party funding impropriety (the Ecclestone affair) and personal sleaze (Geoffrey Robinson, Peter Mandelson and Keith Vaz). However, prior to the 2001 general election, sections of the media broadened their attack to include Blair's style of leadership, his manipulation of Labour's internal candidate selection processes and dishonesty over government policy, principally over so-called 'stealth' taxes and Labour's published spending plans.

In the run-up to the 2001 general election, New Labour's obsession with news management had arguably become counterproductive as journalists filed stories unpacking the spin for their audiences. For some commentators 'spin' was becoming for the Blair premiership what 'sleaze' had been the Major government – a critical label used as shorthand to sum up the perceived deficiencies of an administration. (Kuhn, 2005: 98)

The initial source of the government's difficulties was the extent of the media's reaction once it became wise to Labour's media manipulation (Franklin 2004; Wring 2006). Disgruntled at the ease with which they had been used by Campbell and his acolytes to sell government policy, their journalism became even more 'process' driven and increasingly framed by the accusation that government spinning was now so extensive that very little of the information it released could be taken at face value.

However, the government did not help its cause with the way it responded to these changed circumstances. Too often, its spin doctors continued to allow themselves to become the story, most obviously when Campbell locked horns with Gordon Brown's main media adviser, Charlie Whelan. Whilst Campbell eventually forced Whelan to resign in the aftermath of the **Robinson–Mandelson home loans scandal**, their protracted row only brought into sharper focus the growing animosity between Blair and Brown.

After Labour's election victory, however, the problem began to spiral out of control. Though the government had offered some concessions to its critics in the period 2000–2, its much preferred policy was still to face them down. With hindsight, such defensive aggression was a mistake. Firstly, it led to a 'bunker mentality' within Downing Street, whereby Campbell in particular seems to have convinced himself that sections of the media – with the *Daily Mail* and the BBC at the top of his list – were out to 'get' the prime minister. Campbell was said to be particularly angry over what he saw as the deliberate revival of stories which would have otherwise fallen from the news agenda and which, in his eyes at least, served no purpose other than embarrassing the government. Secondly, it only encouraged the media to watch for evidence of Labour's 'spinning' with even greater intensity (see Box 6.4). The first high-profile victims

Box 6.4 Overspin: Labour's second-term difficulties

The episode which caused Blair the greatest personal difficulty was the so-called Cheriegate affair, which focused on his wife's relations with the boyfriend of her 'style guru', the fraudster Peter Foster. Campbell had originally assured the media that Mrs Blair and Mr Foster were little more than passing acquaintances. However, when evidence came to light that Foster had indeed helped the Blairs purchase property in Bristol for their son's benefit, Campbell brought huge pressure to bear on Mrs Blair, culminating in a tearful television apology. The prime minister, siding quite naturally with his wife, was not impressed with Campbell, who was rumoured to be on the verge of resigning.

More serious were media reports that Downing Street had interfered with 'Black Rod's' arrangements for the funeral of the Queen Mother in order to accord Tony Blair greater personal prominence. Such suggestions were furiously denied by Campbell, who lodged a formal complaint with the Press Complaints Commission. That Campbell eventually backed down only encouraged speculation that the original reports were correct.

However, the most serious of all were the two incidents involving Jo Moore, a special adviser to the most media-conscious of all Blair's Cabinet ministers: Secretary of State for Transport Stephen Byers. Moore had first come to national prominence when a leaked email sent by her famously suggested that al-Qa'aida's attack on the World Trade Center was 'a good day to bury bad news'. Despite the intense feelings Moore's behaviour generated, Campbell and Byers were determined to save her. Yet when the same pattern of behaviour resurfaced against the backdrop of Princess Margaret's funeral, they reluctantly and with evident ill-grace let her go.

Even then, the controversy did not diminish. Firstly, many people could not understand why Moore had been allowed to stay for so long. Secondly, Campbell and Byers found themselves accused of trying to engineer the resignation of the Department's chief information officer, Martin Sixsmith; partly to save face, partly out of revenge.

were Jo Moore, followed by her departmental boss and arch-Blairite, Stephen Byers, who was effectively forced to resign from the Cabinet on 28 May 2002 after a concerted media campaign against him. Worse – much worse – was to follow.

Government, media and wartime reporting

The catalyst was the invasion of Iraq in March 2003. Wartime is a particularly febrile period in government–media relations. Firstly, ministers are even more sensitive to media reporting than usual. Kuhn (2005: 98) notes that 'There is a tendency . . . for governments to believe that at times of military conflict the media should fulfil the function of mobilizing public opinion in support of official policy.' He goes on to add that some sections of the media fall in behind the government's position almost instinctively. Others – especially broadcasters – do not. This can have a powerfully destabilising effect. Margaret Thatcher, for one, never forgave the BBC for its reporting during the 1982 **Falklands War** and the 'Troubles' in Northern Ireland. To her, right was so obviously on one side and absent from the other that she could not understand why the BBC insisted on reporting both positions from a detached, objective perspective. By the time Allied forces invaded Iraq in March 2003, there was strong anecdotal and other evidence that both Blair and Campbell had come to the same view: that a strong anti-war party existed in Broadcasting House who would take every opportunity to discredit the government.

Matters came to a head in the most dramatic fashion in May 2003. The background to this was the growing unease that the government had failed to make a convincing case for war. Tony Blair's fiercest critics suggested that the prime minister's decision to commit British forces was motivated solely by his desire to demonstrate his personal loyalty to the White House. To defend itself from such accusations, the government published two dossiers.

- The first of these, released in September 2002, was a summary of its own intelligence analysis and contained two very important claims: that the Iraqi regime possessed weapons of mass destruction (WMD) and, further, that they could be deployed against British citizens within 45 minutes.
- Later, in February 2003, ministers authorised the publication of the second or 'dodgy' dossier which subsequently turned out to have been plagiarised from a 12-year-old Ph.D. thesis.

Whilst the first of these was the more important, it was the second that ultimately framed the news agenda. That a British government would attempt to pass off a rather aged piece of academic research

Box 6.5 Campbell, Rageh Omar and reporting the Taliban

A famous dispute in 1999 captures the escalating tension between Campbell and the BBC, as well as the clear gap that had opened in respect of their competing news values. During the Allied invasion of Afghanistan, BBC TV reporter Rageh Omar was filmed outside severely damaged buildings which the Taliban claimed had been destroyed by the Allies. Numerous civilians were rumoured to have lost their lives.

This was by no means an uncommon accusation. No doubt this was what persuaded the BBC that this was a legitimate story, highlighting the military and political complexity of modern warfare and the dangers faced by ordinary Afghans. Campbell saw it very differently. In his eyes, this was little more than mischief-making; capitalising on a tragic accident and, by blurring the distinction between an accident of war and systematic repression, thereby giving political comfort to Islamic extremists the world over.

as prime intelligence seemed to confirm that Labour had learned absolutely nothing from the Jo Moore affair. Consequently, when the much-hoped-for evidence of WMD failed to materialise, many voices began to question whether the government had also fabricated the original dossier.

Enter Gilligan

At 6.00 a.m. on 29 May 2003, right in the middle of this highly charged situation, BBC reporter Andrew Gilligan broke the sensational story that a well-placed insider believed that the first dossier had indeed been 'sexed up' at the government's request. Gilligan repeated this accusation in an article in the *Mail on Sunday* three days later, in which he named Campbell as the responsible party. Campbell himself reacted as one might expect, publicly criticising the BBC and demanding an apology at every turn. There followed what Wring (2006: 242) describes as 'a stream of communications between the government and the BBC', culminating in Campbell's uninvited appearance on *Channel 4 News* in which he robustly defended himself and reiterated his criticisms of both the Corporation's journalism and management.

In the meantime, however, a real tragedy was unfolding. On 9 July the Ministry of Defence confirmed to journalists that the source of Gilligan's story was leading weapons expert Dr David Kelly. The following day Dr Kelly was duly named by three national newspapers. Eight days later – after two traumatic appearances before the House of Commons Foreign Affairs Select Committee – he was dead, the formal and much disputed verdict being that he had taken his own life. The government had little alternative but to commission a public inquiry and duly appointed a leading judge, Lord Hutton, to chair it.

In one sense his report, published on 28 January 2004, gave the government everything it might have wished for. Ministers and their officials were completely exonerated of the charge of 'sexing up', whilst the BBC was condemned out of hand for the standard of its journalism. Campbell also had the personal satisfaction of seeing both the BBC chairman and director general resign from post. At the same time, the wider media and public reaction was anything other than comforting. Though the Murdoch press inevitably rounded on the BBC, the majority of the national media condemned Hutton as a government stooge. In addition, because Hutton had gathered much of his evidence in public this had enabled the public to establish a clear idea of culpability some time before the publication of his report. The fact that so much of this evidence confirmed the impression that an unelected official – Campbell – was 'at the centre of all of the important networks deciding British policy on Iraq' (Wring 2006: 245) did little for the government's cause. The net effect of this very sorry affair could be seen during the 2005 general election, when Iraq returned to dominate the campaign (Butler and Kavanagh 2006: 79–80, 109).

A public relations state

However, whilst the Gilligan affair and the death of Dr Kelly had a profound effect on the BBC, government communications carried on very much as before. Campbell resigned, of course. However, despite Blair's protestations that his government had moved beyond 'spin' and his acceptance of the mildly critical Phillis Report (Box 6.6), anecdotal and quantitative evidence strongly suggest that the media machine that Campbell had built continued to operate much as it had always done (Wring 2006: 239).

Box 6.6 The Phillis Report

The controversy over government communications prior to the 2001 general election had persuaded Blair to appoint media executive Bob Phillis to lead an inquiry into information management across Whitehall. Phillis finally reported at more or less the same time as Lord Hutton in January 2004. Some of his findings were critical of practice during the Campbell era. For example, Phillis recommended that:

- a new post – Permanent Secretary for Government Communications – should be created to bring this aspect of the government's work once again under the control of a civil servant rather than a special adviser;
- the post-holder would become the head of a new Government Communications Network (GCN), incorporating both the GICS and the CIO. In other words, never again would these two bodies be led by a paid adviser; and
- whilst the prime minister was free to appoint a separate Director of Communications (Campbell's title when he resigned), this role should be clearly distinguished from that of the permanent secretary.

At the same time, however, Phillis broadly supported the Blair–Campbell analysis that communication was equally as important as policy-making and service delivery. Little wonder, therefore, that neither Blair nor Brown felt under any obligation to dismantle the machine that Campbell had built.

Two related examples will have to suffice. Firstly, concealment was very much in evidence when, on 14 December 2006, Tony Blair became the first prime minister to be interviewed as part of a criminal investigation and three adverse stories were quietly released into the public domain:

- the Serious Fraud Office's decision to drop the investigation into the al-Yamamah bribe scandal;
- Lord Stevens's report into the death of Diana, Princess of Wales; and
- the closure of 2,500 post offices.

Whitehall insiders were rumoured to have described 14 December as 'take out the trash day', a comment which immediately invited comparisons with the government's reaction to 9/11 (Wintour et al. 2006). The SFO's decision to terminate its investigation into BAE's alleged bribery of members of the Saudi royal family to secure an arms contract was particularly significant. This was a highly controversial decision which the OECD (Organisation for Economic Co-operation and Development) refused to accept. When it became clear that the OECD intended to examine the conduct of the British government, the latter produced a dossier to defend its position, claiming that the Saudis had threatened to withdraw intelligence cooperation unless the SFO's investigation was pulled and, further, that the Secret Intelligence Service (MI6) supported this view. Later, however, leaks from within Whitehall and the OECD showed that the head of MI6 had initially refused to sign the dossier, which had been substantially redrafted as a result. The leaks also revealed that MI6 was not convinced that the Saudis would withdraw intelligence cooperation as the government suggested. Coming a mere three years after the publication of the Hutton Report, this affair suggested that, far from learning from their previous errors, ministers preferred to run the risk of being exposed over manipulating intelligence data rather than lose control over the news agenda (Leigh et al. 2007).

This has led to numerous criticisms: short-termism; a disproportionate interest in the prejudices of focus groups; and most damagingly an approach to public relations described by John Major as 'deceit licensed by government' (Wring 2006: 234). The long-term impact of the Blair era has been explored by veteran BBC reporter and 'spin decoder' Nicholas Jones (2007). He is by no means universally critical of Blair and Campbell. Aside from praising Blair's skills as a media performer and the loyalty he showed to his staff, Jones also suggests that many of their reforms were both helpful and long overdue. This was particularly true of the way both men made Whitehall more sensitive to the needs of the media, the opening up of the lobby and Blair's willingness to hold monthly press conferences. However, Jones makes no secret of his view that the disadvantages far outweighed them.

- The ability of the lobby to question government conduct was significantly undermined both by Campbell's bullying and by his persistence in private and selective briefings.

Box 6.7 Government communications under Brown

After a good start, Brown's communication team began to struggle with the demands of running such extensive media management operations. This led to speculation that the people Brown brought with him from the Treasury were suffocating under an avalanche of information which prevented them from exerting any central control. After the public relations disaster in autumn 2007, when both he and his advisers were widely condemned for encouraging speculation that the prime minister may seek a dissolution, Brown reorganised his team early in January 2008. The appointment of PR executive Stephen Carter to the new post of Chief of Strategy and Principal Adviser attracted much comment, not least because it was presented by some commentators as a panic move.

Jeremy Heywood: permanent secretary at 10 Downing Street
Michael Ellam: prime minister's official spokesman
Stephen Carter: chief of strategy

Sue Nye :	Nicola Burdett:	David Muir:	Deborah Mattison:	Damien McBride:
director of government relations	'gaffe manager'	director of strategy	principal pollster	media manager

As events transpired, Carter's appointment was not a happy one. Within two months it had become an open secret within Whitehall that his presence was a source of division (Hinsliff 2008). Eventually, in October 2008, Carter left his post in Downing Street to take up the position of Minister of Communications, Technology and Broadcasting, with Brown's principal media manager moving to a 'back room' role at the same time. In April 2009, as we have seen in Chapter 3, McBride's career was finished when he was forced to resign in the aftermath of the 'Red Rag' scandal (see Box 3.2). By this point, in a further sign of Brown's increasing nervousness, Peter Mandelson was back in government and Alastair Campbell rumoured to be working behind the scenes.

- The reputation of government information officers was sullied and is yet to recover.
- Parliament's reputation as the nation's principal political forum has been completely lost, possibly forever.
- Worse, journalists themselves were corrupted by Campbell's brutal manipulation of their quest for exclusives, as a result of which they were too often reduced to 'the eager beneficiaries of the government's largesse in trailing decisions'.

Equally, however, Jones sees no reason to believe that any government, regardless of its political complexion, will readily give up the advantages the public relations state can bring (see also Silver 2007). This is very evident from the behaviour of the Brown government. Despite repeating Tony Blair's pledge to move on from the age of spin, his government was immediately dogged by accusations that it was hewn from exactly the same political material (Brown 2007). That Alastair Campbell subsequently confirmed that he had also accepted a position as a communications adviser to Downing Street (*Daily Mail*, 17 October 2008) and, later, that he had turned down the offer of running Labour's next general election campaign (Murphy 2009) only adds to this sense of déjà vu.

According to Wring (2006: 231), the net effect has been the creation of the public relations state, 'a behind-the-scenes, often largely secretive, network of spin doctors, communications directors and political aides who communicate with print and broadcast journalists on behalf of the government they serve.'

Whilst commentators will argue for some time yet over its integrity and constitutionality, one thing is clear: the emergence of the public relations state makes Clement Attlee's vision of a government policy on communications aimed at raising political consciousness and encouraging active participation in public life a dusty relic of a world long since lost.

Conclusion

This chapter has attempted to show two things: how government communications have evolved and why this process has provoked such passionate argument. It also reaffirms the broad thrust of Chapter 5:

that media management is so important in contemporary political communications that it has swept aside many of the restraining barriers which might have kept it in check. We have a decent idea what it is politicians hope to gain from mediated communications, but this alone does not explain why they have patently come to see the media as an enemy to be vanquished. This is the question which will shape the next two chapters, via which I hope to place media management in its proper analytical context.

What you should have learnt from reading this chapter

- How government communications developed prior to 1997.
- The reasons why Tony Blair and Alastair Campbell were determined to introduce reform and how they set about doing this.
- Why their reforms were subsequently discredited by events.
- The significance of the concept of a public relations state .

Glossary of key terms

Falklands War On 2 April 1982, the Argentine government ordered its forces to invade the Falkland Islands, officially owned by the UK since 1833 but claimed by Argentina. One month later – on 1 May – Argentine and UK forces engaged in combat for the first time in what turned out to be a six-week conflict culminating in the surrender of the former on 14 June.

Robinson–Mandelson home loans scandal Peter Mandelson's first ministerial resignation occurred after he was accused of making misleading claims over personal finances, especially his financial relations with fellow minister Geoffrey Robinson. The complicating factor was that Mandelson's department was conducting an investigation into Robinson's business dealings at the same time as Mandelson owed him a considerable amount of money.

The 'project' The term used by New Labour insiders to describe their vision for the transformation of the Labour party and centre-left politics.

Andy Wood A high-profile information officer who was sacked from his post in the Northern Ireland Office in the early years of the Blair government. Wood's dismissal was one of the first incidents to draw media attention to the replacement of long-serving professional civil servants with outsiders.

Likely examination questions

Why and how did the Blair government reform government communications between 1997 and 2001?

Why and for what reasons did Alastair Campbell's conduct as chief press secretary and later director of government communications generate so much controversy?

Explain why the concept of a public relations state might be seen as a threat to the conduct of public life in the UK.

 Helpful websites

A history of the Central Information Office can be found at www.cio.gov. uk. The Cabinet Office and an important link to all aspects of government communication can be located at www.cabinetoffice.gov.uk, whilst the 10 Downing Street media centre is at www.number10.gov.uk.

Suggestions for further reading

This is one area of political communication where the reader is wonderfully well served by a wealth of excellent material. The first and third chapters of Bob Franklin's *Packaging Politics* offer a highly accessible account of the main tools available to ministers as they seek to manage the media. For those of you interested in the legal and constitutional aspects of government relations with the media, Geoffrey Robertson and Andrew Nichol's 2008 *Media Law* (London: Penguin) remains the outstanding work of reference. There are numerous sources offering a very helpful insight into New Labour's attitude to the media, though I have drawn heavily on John Bartle 'The Labour government and the media' in J. Bartle and A. King (eds), *Britain at the Polls 2005* (Washington, DC: CQ Press, 2006). Chapter 2 of Franklin's *Packaging Politics* (2004) summarises the reforms to government communication brought about under New Labour, as does Margaret Scammell 'Media and Media Management' in A. Seldon (ed.), *The Blair Effect* (London: Little, Brown, 2001) and Raymond Kuhn 'Media Management' in Seldon and Kavanagh (eds), *The Blair Effect 2001–5* (Cambridge: Cambridge University Press, 2005, pp. 94–111). A good introduction to the concept of the public relations state can be found in Dominic Wring 'The News Media and the Public Relations State' in P. Dunleavy et al. (eds), *Developments in British Politics 8* (Basingstoke: Palgrave, 2006).

Media Bias

Contents

Overview

In the previous two chapters we saw the remarkable lengths to which British politicians go in order to secure a favourable media coverage. One explanation for this is the belief, common to all politicians, that the media are routinely and systematically biased against them. Consequently, this chapter examines what politicians might mean when describing the media in this way. In doing so, it will argue that, in order to fully appreciate its extent and significance, a wider and more flexible definition is required than the rather basic model of overt partisanship associated with the behaviour of the tabloid press.

Key issues to be covered in this chapter

- The several and distinctive meanings of bias
- The changing patterns of partisanship within the print media
- The importance of the concepts of 'genre' and 'frame' in understanding media bias
- The nature and importance of propaganda bias
- The 'bad news' studies and ideological bias

Deconstructing the concept

In recent years, interest in media bias has reached a point where one might be forgiven for thinking that it is 'the only important issue in the relationship between politics and mass media' (Street 2001: 15). Certainly, it is the one topic which consistently and persistently arouses the passions of politicians and has been used to excuse their own behaviour when the latter has fallen below a standard the electorate might have a right to expect.

Market failure
Our understanding of this relationship is shaped by a powerful set of assumptions about the media's wider role in a democratic polity. These draw heavily on a derivation of the economic theory of **market failure**. Given that the vast majority of political information flows through the media before its reaches the electorate, it follows that partial and inaccurate reporting on the former's part could distort political outcomes. This is particularly so where convention encourages voters to believe that journalists endeavour to report the news accurately and with a view to providing a balanced coverage of competing viewpoints.

As John Street (2001: 18) explains, however, there is a strong argument that media reporting will always fall short of the ideal type. In the first instance, a number of important structural constraints will always prevent journalists from giving a full account of a news story:

- There is a seemingly infinite number of possible news stories and only a limited amount of space (and time) available to cover them.
- Journalists within each news organisation will seek to promote their own favoured storylines, thereby placing additional pressure on editors to make difficult choices between competing news items.
- The intense pressure to produce stories before agreed deadlines restricts still further the resources that can be devoted to news-gathering.
- Commercial pressures mean that long, factual accounts are avoided to protect a media organisation's position in the battle for circulation/ratings.

- Within each story there are simply too many facts to be recorded and too many opinions to be balanced against each other. Of necessity, therefore, journalists will adopt what Street calls a 'criterion of relevance' to help choose between them.
- Finally, those facts and opinions which are covered have to be moulded into 'a story with a narrative that links them together'. This is essential if the story is to prove attractive to the intended audience.

As a result, journalists and their editors have reorganised their working practices to help assist in the selection of their materials and the construction of their narratives. Nor are these by any means uniform. Indeed, one of the other key decisions journalists have to take when selecting and evaluating their news items is the extent to which their organisations encourage them to be objective or expect their reporting to be given a deliberate 'slant'. In this context, the views of proprietors, editors, advertisers and audiences can all play a crucial role in the construction of bias, an issue which we shall examine in more detail in the penultimate chapter.

Typologies of bias

These factors support the idea that bias of sorts is endemic to journalism. In turn, this has led academic observers to construct more rigorous typologies of bias to help us understand the complexities of this concept. To illustrate this point, the remainder of this chapter will draw heavily on Denis McQuail's four-part framework (see Box 7.1). McQuail uses two criteria –whether the bias is explicit (overt) or implicit and whether it is deliberate or unintended – to identify four different types of bias. This approach suggests very strongly that the concept of media bias is both more interesting and more challenging than might otherwise appear to be the case.

Partisan bias: the case of the British press

Media bias is most commonly understood in terms of the partisanship consistently shown by British newspapers. The lack of a powerful regulatory framework for British newspapers means that the latter are free to be as overtly partisan as they see fit. This is particularly

Box 7.1 A typology of bias

Partisan bias is both explicit and deliberate and is often linked to clear editorial advice on matters of political choice or controversy.

In partial contrast, *propaganda bias* uses a range of devices – imagery, language, tone - to encourage the audience to make value judgements about the story's subject. This form of bias is equally keen for readers or viewers to draw very particular conclusions yet seeks to keep this fact well hidden.

Unwitting bias is explicit in its content but is not intended to lead the audience towards pre-determined outcomes. The most obvious example of this is the choice and ordering of news stories, including the all-important 'lead' item. It should be added, though, that this seemingly innocuous form of bias can generate dramatic responses among spin doctors, many of whom will interpret the manner in which stories are prioritised as another form of propaganda bias.

Ideological bias is neither explicit nor intended. Instead, it structures reporting around certain values or 'norms'. These are dominated by a journalist's perceptions of how people are likely to react to a particular story and tend to reinforce popular beliefs and prejudices about their subjects.

marked at election time and is invariably reflected in the choice of front-page headlines and editorial opinion. From an analytical perspective, this type of bias poses few problems largely because it is both overt and intended. Further, most mainstream politicians accept it as a fact of political life and factor it into their communication strategies accordingly.

Dealignment of the press

However, this does not mean that overt partisanship among British newspapers is disregarded by academic opinion. On the contrary, in recent years three developments in particular have caused academic observers to reconsider a number of widely accepted beliefs about the nature and patterns of press bias. The first of these questions whether press bias is as important as it once was. Newspaper

Table 7.1 Newspaper interest in general elections (figures refer to the number of front-page leads on the election campaign)

Paper	1992 (25 days' campaigning)	1997 (27 days' campaigning)	2001 (21 days' campaigning)	2005 (21 days' campaigning)
Sun	9	6	9	7
Mirror	13	13	12	7
Star	5	1	4	2
Mail	18	14	9	12
Express	19	14	2	11
Telegraph	24	25	15	16
Times	25	25	18	16
Guardian	23	23	15	18
Independent	20	17	17	15
Financial Times	22	21	17	18

circulation is in serious, possibly even terminal, decline. With an ever-widening range of alternative sources at their disposal, it is questionable whether a typical 'post-modern' voter will take much notice of traditional Fleet Street tub-thumping. This is even more so when one notes the remarkable lack of attention some titles give to election campaigns, a point which, as we noted in Chapter 4, has undoubtedly influenced the placing of party advertisements.

At the same time, however, there is also an important complicating factor at work: the power certain titles have to 'buck the trend'. This is certainly the case with *The Sun* and the *Daily Mail*, a factor compounded by the fact that these papers are favoured by the most electorally significant voting groups. It is by no means coincidental that New Labour's media management strategy was and in so many respects is still dominated by the need to secure the support of these two papers.

The second development concerns the growing tendency of some newspapers to switch allegiance between elections. With the exception of the decision of Rupert Murdoch to move *The Sun* and *News of the World* into the pro-Conservative camp in the 1970s, newspaper allegiance had been relatively stable. However, as the list below indicates, beginning in 1992 this pattern began to change:

- Firstly, during the campaign itself four of the eleven dailies heavily qualified their support or refused it altogether.
- Secondly, in the aftermath of '**Black Wednesday**' John Major was largely abandoned by the pro-Conservative press, the exception being the *Daily Express*. Though some titles returned to the Conservative fold in time for the next general election, others did not. Sensing the dissatisfaction, Tony Blair and his media advisers made a concerted attempt to win over the waverers. Whilst their efforts were by no means universally successful, they did secure one remarkable coup when Rupert Murdoch brought *The Sun* and later the *News of the World* into the pro-Blair camp.
- However, the shift towards Labour should not be interpreted as signs of a mass conversion to the Labour cause. One reason is that much of the support for Labour was highly conditional. In addition, however, a number of titles including the dominant mid-market tabloids the *Daily Mail* and *Mail on Sunday* proved impervious to Labour's charm offensive. Perhaps most significantly, some of the 'converts' subsequently switched back to the Conservatives after Labour's political troubles in the aftermath of military intervention in Afghanistan and Iraq. This is most obviously so in the case of the Express Group and suggests that a further haemorrhage of support may follow prior to the general election scheduled for 2010, the more so given *The Sun*'s well-publicised declaration for David Cameron's Conservatives in September 2009.

The impact of shifting allegiance has been compounded by a third factor: the absence of coherent partisanship *within* a newspaper. This operates on numerous levels:

- There is an unprecedented tolerance among editors for their star correspondents and columnists to express often markedly different views to those contained in their newspaper's editorials

Table 7.2 Changing patterns of newspaper bias

Paper	1992	1997	2001	2005
Sun	Staunchly pro-Conservative – though it actually paid less attention to the election than any other newspaper with the exception of the Star.	Stridently pro-Labour – the most remarkable and remarked-upon switch in allegiance in living memory.	Still supportive of Labour – but in a further sign of the instability of its partisanship it actually promoted a pro-Conservative agenda on particular issues.	Labour – but essentially supportive of Blair rather than his party.
Mirror	Labour – but 'old' rather than 'new' in its coverage of certain issues.	Labour – but in an upbeat manner not seen in 1992.	Labour – but with a resigned air that the election was a foregone conclusion.	Labour – but with considerable reservations over government foreign policy and Blair's leadership.
Star	Officially non-partisan – but dismissive of both Labour and the Liberal Democrats	Labour – but only at the very end of the campaign. Once again, the least interested of the papers.	Labour – but, as in 1997, in a decidedly lukewarm manner.	Non-partisan – but with a notable anti-Labour bias in its reporting.

Table 7.2 (continued)

Paper	1992	1997	2001	2005
Mail	*Conservative* – but critical of John Major's leadership and, surprisingly perhaps, appreciative of Neil Kinnock's attempts to change the Labour party.	*Conservative* – but essentially anti-Blair – real interest lay in coverage of UK–EU relations, which only added to John Major's discomfort.	*Conservative* – but without any obvious enthusiasm.	*Conservative* – but, as in 1997, the main focus of its reporting was anti-Labour and especially anti-Blair.
Express	Staunchly pro-*Conservative* – worked with Conservative campaign managers to turn floating voters away from the Liberal Democrats.	*Conservative* – but without any of the exuberance it had shown in 1992.	*Labour* – but in reality, pro-Blair. By far the least committed of the papers.	*Conservative* – and with the same level of enthusiasm seen in 1992.
Telegraph	*Conservative* – the most pro-Tory of the qualities, though, like the *Mail*, with obvious reservations over John Major's leadership.	*Conservative* – once again the most committed paper in its support of John Major	*Conservative* – the most overtly hostile of all the national dailies to the Labour party.	*Conservative* – but concerns over Tory policy on Iraq and immigration ensured that its support was markedly less enthusiastic than in 1997 and 2001

Times	Conservative – but by no means as enthusiastically as *The Telegraph*.	Non-partisan – for the first time since 1966	Labour – but ironically as the party best placed to consolidate Thatcherism!	Labour (just) – the paper was clear that it also wanted a large and influential Conservative opposition.
Guardian	Labour – the only quality to back the main opposition party, though with considerable unease about Neil Kinnock's leadership.	Labour – though with more enthusiasm than in 1992.	Labour – but now with obvious reservations.	Labour – but with heavy qualifications. As the campaign wore on, its reporting actually focused on those issues which most harmed Blair.
Independent	Non-partisan – deliberately positioned itself as an objective and detached observer.	Labour – for the first time in its history, *The Independent* backed a political party. However, it also advocated a strong Liberal Democrat presence.	Non-partisan – but with clear hostility to the Conservatives.	Non-partisan – but highly supportive of large gains in the number of Liberal Democrat MPs. Like *The Guardian*, its coverage of individual issues was anti-Blair.
Financial Times	Labour – but only as the largest party in a hung parliament.	Labour – but ambiguously and with little enthusiasm for Blair.	Labour – though again with qualifications.	Labour – largely because it posed no obvious threat to business interests.

- This trend is replicated within newspaper groups. For example, Mr Murdoch's willingness to bring the influence of *The Sun* and *News of the World* to bear on Tony Blair's fortunes was not matched by an equal determination to reposition the upmarket *Times* and *Sunday Times*.
- Newspapers are also willing to grant or withdraw support depending upon a party's stance on particular issues. In some cases, most obviously *The Times* in 1997, partisanship can become exclusively 'issues orientated'
- More generally, partisanship has become increasingly conditional, both in respect of a party's policy position and the person occupying its leadership.

There is, in short, little to suggest that changing allegiance is underpinned by ideological conversion. Unsurprisingly, Tony Blair's career as leader of the Labour party exemplifies this. Detailed textual analyses of the press confirm that the surge in support for Labour was more or less exclusively about Blair and not his party. To repeat what has become something of a cliché, the Tory press had been replaced by the 'Tony press'. The question facing his successor, of course, is the extent to which he will be able to retain such support in very different political circumstances. One suspects that, as a result, the last chapter on press dealignment is still to be written.

Propaganda bias

'Propaganda bias' refers to the ability of the media to shape public attitudes in ways which disguise their intentions. To understand how this might happen, however, we must first explore two additional concepts: the 'frame' and the 'genre'. The first of these is used to explain both how journalists select their stories from the multiple events happening more or less simultaneously and how they highlight certain features of their chosen event in order to create their *narratives*. According to Street (2001: 44) the selection of a frame will be heavily influenced by the genre in which a journalist is working. This refers to a host of conventions and expectations that shape the media's responses to the events on which they report. These include:

- The commercial nature of a particular news organisation, its competition for circulation and ratings and its need to link an audience to advertisers. Street argues that these 'commercial imperatives' have grown much stronger in recent years and have also come to influence non-commercial organisations such as the BBC.
- The commercial importance of treating news reporting rather like any other media commodity. This means that a new emphasis has been placed on presenting it in a 'user-friendly' format, one which is shorter, visually attractive, hi-tech and focused on lifestyle and human interest as far as this is possible.
- Anticipated audience reactions: what the latter will expect from a particular story and the conventions which duly govern its presentation. National cultural traditions will be very important in this respect, which journalists seeking to win audience ratings will need to consider and appease.

The net effect is that journalists working within a particular genre will draw on its assumptions to select the appropriate 'frame' in which to present their stories. One can gain a sense of this from Box 7.2.

Box 7.2 'Framing' news items	
Story	**Typical frame**
The conduct of representative assemblies	Soap opera, light entertainment
Election contests	Mighty clashes between rival leaders, sporting contests (horse races)
Appointment/election of young party leaders	Galvanising an inert party
Political behaviour	The product of the activity of key individuals
Political motives	Devotion to principle (idealists) or strategic consideration (careerists)

(*Source:* Street 2001: 47–53)

Newspapers, propaganda bias and the reporting of salient political issues

However, it is also the case that 'frames' can be used in the reporting of particular policy areas. Kuhn (2007: 160–1) uses the issues of crime and European integration to show how certain newspapers have framed issues in ways which play on popular fears and prejudices and significantly limit the policy options available to governments. For example, he cites research which shows how the press routinely focus disproportionate attention on violent crime, including crimes of sexual violence, in ways which 'may give audiences a skewed picture of the potential threat'. It is perhaps not merely coincidental that left-leaning politicians no longer believe that a general election can be won where a party is perceived as being 'soft' on crime, hence the general preference for populist policies which, whilst they possess very limited practical value, have enormous political appeal (Foster 1999). This might also explain one of the great paradoxes in modern criminology: government's willingness to allow the prison population to rise to record levels at a time when, according to its own figures, the crime rate is falling. Similarly press coverage of the European Union has been framed largely by a powerful Euroscepticism, evident in 'pieces ridiculing decisions by the European Commission to articles praising the defence of "British" values and practices in the face of alleged external threats' (Kuhn 2007: 161). The effect, according to at least one prominent critic, has been to place policy on future UK–EU relations in the hands of certain best-selling newspaper groups – News International and Associated – whose reporting almost defies politicians to adopt a pro-European stance (Garton Ash 2004).

Commentators are also concerned by the framing of political issues in ways which draw audience attention away from detailed but complex explanations in favour of the crude but simplistic. This is often compounded by the way in which frames of this type invariably invite audiences to draw the most sweeping and generalised conclusions from individual cases. This is captured in the recent press reporting of Toorpaki Saiedi, an Afghan refugee living with her seven children in a house worth £1.2 million, for which Ealing Council were paying to its owners a rent of £12,000 per month. Two things are particularly noteworthy here. Firstly, the reporting focused exclusively on the alleged incompetence of three council officials as the cause of what the press saw as a scandalous waste of public resources. At no point was the dearth of suitable council-owned property considered as a factor, or the attitude of private landlords who were quite willing to charge such an inordinate sum to the public purse. Secondly, the reporting seemed to uncritically reaffirm public anxiety over large immigrant families draining local authorities of much-needed cash. In his coverage of the media reporting, Peter Wilby (2008) quotes the sociologist W. G. Runciman to the effect that the focus of our anger and envy is always on the person next door. By focusing solely on the Saiedi family's current circumstances – little or nothing was mentioned of those which led them to leave Afghanistan for the UK – it can be argued that the press was simply feeding the widespread and historic resentment of the British to newcomers living in their midst.

This type of reporting has attracted much comment. Street (2001: 23) notes how semiotics emerged in the 1960s precisely in order to show the 'way meaning is contained in what is not said as well as what is, in images and impressions as much as in words'. More pertinently, he also refers to the work of John Thompson (1988) who has demonstrated some of the linguistic techniques which can be used to covertly communicate bias. The reader will no doubt make the appropriate connections with the Saiedi case.

- *Legitimisation:* attaching an 'expert' opinion to endorse a highly contested viewpoint.
- *Dissimulation:* disguising complex social causes by blaming fallible individuals.
- *Fragmentation:* presenting different groups (for example, poor whites and poor immigrants in search of decent public housing) as if they have irreconcilable differences, when the very opposite is in fact the case.
- *Reification:* presenting the world as fixed, with no plausible case for change.

For left-wingers, the use of such techniques to support propaganda bias among the more popular newspapers places them under a permanent disadvantage. However, they also argue that this would matter less if there were still a significant number of popular left-leaning titles to offer an alternative view. It remains a consider-able source of frustration that efforts to revive the radical press in the UK have foundered for lack of financial resources. We shall see in Chapter 9 how this has shaped left-wing demands for sweeping reform of government policy on newspaper ownership.

Broadcasters, propaganda bias and the neo-conservatives

Left-wing commentators have been equally active in their attacks on a propaganda bias among broadcasters (Curran and Seaton 2003). However, it is worth noting that neo-conservatives have also been very vocal in this area, particularly in attacking the frames allegedly used by the BBC. These, or so they argue, perpetuate a metropolitan, elitist and above all liberal world view at the expense of those values which are supported by the overwhelming majority of the BBC's viewers and listeners.

These criticisms should be distinguished from the historic animos-ity shown towards the BBC by the Thatcher and Major governments. This was complicated by the particular issue of war reporting, though it is worth noting that Lady Thatcher argued that the BBC's war cov-erage exploited the Corporation's legal obligation to be impartial as a fig leaf behind which it could hide its anti-Conservative and anti-British bias. By contrast, later neo-conservatives have aimed their fire over a much wider range of reporting. An excellent recent example of this can be found in Paul Dacre's **Cudlipp Lecture** for 2007 (Dacre 2007).

> [B]y and large BBC journalism starts from the premise of left-wing ideology: it is hostile to conservatism and the traditional right, Britain's past and British values, America, Ulster Unionism, Euroscepticism, capitalism and big business, the countryside, Christianity and family values.

Quite a list! According to Dacre, the BBC's left-wing propaganda bias is framed through a wide range of techniques including 'the choice of stories, the way they are angled, the choice of interviewees and, most pertinently, the way those interviewees are treated'. Dacre is particularly concerned over the latter. He argues that the result is a dismissal of those who do not share the BBC's metropolitan elitism as 'sexist, racist, fascist or judgemental'. The result has been to 'shut down' a wide range of important debates – Dacre mentions education, health, immigration and law and order – as would-be contributors modify their comments to avoid labelling and ridicule.

Readers can decide for themselves whether Mr Dacre's criticisms ring true. However, the neo-conservative critique possesses a political significance which exceeds its technical accuracy, for it has come to play an important part in the rapidly evolving debate on reforming broadcasting content regulations. This has been led by Rupert Murdoch, who argues that the only way the BBC's covert left-liberal bias can be countered is to allow his Sky News to adopt an overtly pro-conservative stance in its news coverage. Recent developments would suggest that Mr Murdoch's thinking is now beginning to influence Conservative party policy, something which could, if given legislative expression by a future Tory government, lead to the most dramatic changes in broadcast policy since the BBC was first granted its Charter in 1926.

Media bias: Tony Blair and the feral pack

However, the most interesting aspect of the current debate on media bias – one which transcends the boundaries of propaganda and unwitting bias – was initiated by Tony Blair. In his lecture on public life, given to an audience at Canary Wharf on 12 June 2007, Blair presented a picture of media bias which was wholly indiscriminate (Blair 2007). It did not seek to undermine particular parties or ideologies so much as politicians themselves. Blair's argument was detailed and closely reasoned. His key point concerned the way in which the established media – newspapers and broadcasters – have reacted to the unprecedented competitive pressure it now faces. Consequently, in order to report the news in ways which are likely to prove commercially attractive, they have devised a three-part strategy: break stories that shape news schedules, provide comment and do so as quickly as technology permits. The combined effect is that the media has fuelled public cynicism and created an environment in which politicians find it virtually impossible to function effectively.

Whilst some journalists broadly supported Blair's comments (Toynbee 2007), the reaction of the majority was dismissive (Wheatcroft 2007). The key accusation, perhaps inevitably, was that Blair was using the media as a scapegoat to explain and more importantly justify the conduct of his own government. Readers are invited to take a view on this. However, Blair's conclusion – that this type of 'anti-politics' propaganda bias has had a seriously detrimental effect on the conduct of public life – is an important point of departure for what is now a highly pertinent public debate. Blair's concerns correspond with academic opinion and also reflect those of a number of prominent journalists (Lloyd 2004). Its validity and the implications for media policy will be examined in much detail in Chapters 8 and 10.

Ideological bias: the 'Bad News' studies

The concepts of the frame and the genre are also highly pertinent to our final example of media bias. Indeed, the affinity of the two concepts, together with the difficulties in distinguishing between human intent and structural factors as the key motivation in covert bias, continues to provide researchers with numerous methodological problems. However, beginning in the 1970s, the Glasgow University Media Group (GUMG) published a series of studies which became known as the 'Bad News' studies, which if nothing else help to draw out the fundamental distinctions between propaganda and ideological bias. These concentrated on the manner in which television broadcasters reported on a variety of controversial topics, beginning with industrial relations and extending to business, the economy and, later, defence. Though elements of the research used qualitative techniques such as semiotics, the key to the studies was a series of highly detailed content analyses. In addition to the language of the news reports, the researchers also examined a variety of other phenomena, including camera angle, presentational format, the type of people interviewed and the settings which formed the backdrop to them.

Their conclusion was that television news reporting was systematically biased in ways which reinforced what Street (2001: 25) calls the 'basic assumptions about society'. Paraphrasing the work of Stevenson (1995), Kuhn (2007: 162) notes that the bias identified by the GUMG operated at three levels:

> . . . first, the media are biased in their representation of social 'reality'; second, television news can be described as biased according

Box 7.3 The 'Bad News' studies

- *Bad News* (1976)
- *More Bad News* (1980)
- *Really Bad News* (1982)
- *War and Peace News* (1985)

to the extent to which it reaffirms or leaves unquestioned the central economic relations of capitalism; third, the news bias involves the exclusion of working class voices from the media of mass communication.

The list of examples which could be cited to illustrate this argument is a long one. However, in the interests of economy, one will have to suffice. This concerns the debate on the causes of inflation. This was the most salient political issue during the 1970s and early 1980s, not least because it impacted heavily on popular attitudes to Conservative economic policy and responsibility for unemployment. The GUMG detected that, without ever explicitly stating this, the content of TV news reports consistently presented inflation as a consequence of 'excessive' and hence unjustified wage demands. This is a highly contested view, but it dovetailed perfectly with a powerful current of political and public opinion that blamed adverse economic phenomena squarely on the trade unions.

Interestingly, Street (2001: 26–7) points out that the GUMG did not conclude that this bias was deliberate, hence the use of the descriptor 'ideological' rather than 'propaganda'. On the contrary, it was the product of habit, tradition and newsroom practice, which combined to ensure that news reporting reflected rather than challenged majoritarian viewpoints. This offers a partial contrast with the enormously influential research conducted by Hernan and Chomsky (1988) into ideological bias among the US print media. The latter concentrated on the reporting of key foreign policy issues during the Carter and Reagan presidencies. Whilst these authors also detected a systematic bias – notably a remarkable consistency between news coverage and the interests of corporate America – they offered a very different explanation as to its causes: the steady absorption of the US media into the mainstream corporate world. Accordingly, the key feature of political communication in the US since 1945 was 'the adaptation of personnel to the constraints of ownership, organisation, market and political power' (1988: xii). Consequently, Hernan and Chomsky argue that, as a result, US media organisations simply adopted the mindset and outlook of the corporations who owned them, to a point where their content automatically assimilated the latter's world view.

The notion of ideological bias is controversial and has by no means been accepted by mainstream academic opinion (Street 2001: 30–2). The GUMG studies in particular were severely criticised by other academic commentators on numerous grounds, not least the variety of methodological problems which they claim compromised the data compiled. The reader is subsequently advised to bear this in mind when evaluating the concept of ideological bias. All the same, the work of the Glasgow researchers marks an important contribution to our understanding of media bias, not least because it adds still further to the argument that the political impartiality demanded by the regulations governing broadcast news is no longer possible. More recently, BBC executives and some of its leading reporters have acknowledged that an innate bias in its news and current affairs coverage is a distinct possibility. However, in marked contrast to the GUMG studies, their fears are that this bias is liberal rather than conservative in orientation. In particular, an internal BBC report into programme-making (*From Seesaw to Wagon Wheel*) admitted that some of its coverage on issues such as world poverty and environmental degradation effectively closed off the possibility that conservative viewpoints could be effectively aired within individual programmes (Gibson 2007a). Unsurprisingly, this admission was seized upon by the Conservative party to justify the debate it wishes to promote on the future of media content regulations.

Conclusion

The purpose of this chapter has not been to debate whether or not the media is biased. The reader is reminded of Street's opening analysis that bias of some sort is endemic in journalism. Instead, the questions I have posed and, at least in part, tried to answer concern the nature of media bias, the manner in which it might differ between news organisations and, most importantly, the different theories which have arisen to explain it. The suggestions for further reading below, together with the several references to academic works in the text itself, should point readers in the right direction to deepen their understanding. If nothing else, it is my hope that Chapter 7 will have gone some way to explain why politicians obsess about media management in the way that they do. In order to complete this explanation I now turn in the next chapter to the complementary issue of media effects.

. . . .

✔ What you should have learnt from reading this chapter

- Something of the different ways in which it is possible to conceptualise media bias.

- Why some commentators talk of a dealignment among the British press.

- How the concepts of the 'frame' and 'genre' explain the distinctive meanings of propaganda and ideological bias.

- The various critiques of media bias from across the political spectrum.

🔍 Glossary of key terms

'Black Wednesday' The name given to the events of 16 September 1992 when the Conservative government was forced to withdraw sterling from membership of the European Exchange Rate Mechanism. For some analysts, this humiliating climbdown marked the beginning of the end for John Major.

Cudlipp Lecture A prestigious annual lecture first given in 2005, in honour of celebrated journalist Hugh Cudlipp.

Market failure The idea that markets depend upon the free and unrestricted flow of information from firms to consumers. Where these information flows fail, markets will cease to function properly.

❓ Likely examination questions

In what ways are the media biased?

Explain the theory of the 'dealignment of the press'.

Can Tony Blair's critique of a 'feral media' be supported by the evidence?

Helpful websites

The Glasgow University Media Group has a website at www.gla.ac.uk/centres/mediagroup. The iconic figure of Noam Chomsky also has an official website, at www.chomsky.info.

Suggestions for further reading

The opening two chapters of John Street's *Mass Media, Politics and Democracy* (Basingstoke: Palgrave, 2001) offer an invaluable analysis of media bias and the challenges it poses for academic commentators. This should be read in conjunction with Chapter 6 of Kuhn's *Politics and the Media in Britain*. Media bias is also discussed at length throughout Curran and Seaton's classic history of the media in Britain: *Power Without Responsibility* (London: Routledge, 2003).

Media Power and Media Effects: Theories and Realities

Contents

Overview

In addition to fears over media bias, the evolution of party political communications reflects a widespread belief that the media plays a vital part in shaping political outcomes. This is especially so in respect of elections, during which the main protagonists devote huge resources to their campaigns in the hope of exploiting media influence. Some academics question the accuracy of this view; others, however, do not and argue that the media has a wide-ranging effect both on politics and political society. Chapter 8 explores the reasons for such contrasting viewpoints and their implications for our understanding of political communication.

Key issues to be covered in this chapter

- The principal trends in media influence research
- The enduring debate among **psephologists** over the media's impact on voting behaviour
- The wider influence of the media on the conduct of politics and public life

Media effects: some general theories

Like politicians, academics have shown a huge interest in the media's ability to influence the attitudes and behaviour of ordinary people, especially in their capacity as voters. It is easy to see why: 'During the course of the day, the average person will devote almost seven hours to watching television, listening to radio, reading a newspaper or scanning the web for news, information or entertainment' (Franklin 2004: 205). While television is a seemingly all-powerful medium, Bill Jones (2004: 202–6) reminds us of the possible impact of newspapers, especially the tabloids.

- They still sell by the million, with an actual readership considerably in excess of their circulation figures. A good example of this is provided by *The Sun*. At a time when its sales stood at 3.2 million, *Sun* executives claimed a readership of 8.5 million, over two-and-a-half times higher.
- Secondly, the tabloids have become increasingly adept at catering for their readers' tastes. Indeed, the very 'lightness' of the more popular titles' political coverage means that voters may be more inclined either to read them regardless of their editorial policies.
- Further, whether or not they can actually shape voter attitudes, the tabloids have an uncanny knack of directing voters' attention to issues which politicians would much prefer them not to think about. As Jones remarks: 'even if a vote is bought through blackening a politician's name, it counts as much as any other on election day'.
- Finally, they have established an important relationship with broadcasters. Though rivals in certain respects, the news journalists working with these different media will also collaborate with one another. Their tendency to work as a 'pack' has been remarked upon earlier in this study. Consequently, politicians and their campaign managers will be very aware that a powerful story published by a newspaper will shape that particular news cycle for all other media organisations.

However, neither these nor similar observations can support the all-important assertion that the media has a significant effect on political outcomes. One very obvious reason is that the average of

Box 8.1 Competing models of media influence

- 1920–30s: 'Magic bullets', 'hypodermics' and 'hammers' (the propaganda model)
- 1940s: The 'two-step' theory
- 1950s–60s: Uses and gratifications (the minimal effects or partisan reinforcement model)
- 1970s–80s: Coding and decoding (empowered participant model)

(*Source:* Franklin 2004; Kuhn, 2007)

seven hours consuming media products will be spent on a range of purposes, most obviously entertainment. Secondly, both concentration levels and audience responses are likely to vary significantly in line with a host of social and cultural factors. How, therefore, can academic researchers be confident that they understand the type of audience with which they are dealing? Will they be media-obsessed **'couch potatoes'**, passively and uncritically absorbing anything put before them; or discerning post-modernists only taking from the media those items they want? Thirdly, even the most fervent advocates of a media effect have to acknowledge that individual behaviour, including voting behaviour, is influenced by a variety of factors. How, therefore, might a research project set about isolating a media from other effects? Worse, even where a measurable convergence in media and voter attitudes can be detected, cause and effect has to be accounted for. For example, it might be just as plausible to argue that the media are following rather than shaping public responses. This is particularly likely in respect of the tabloid press whose marketing strategies lead to editorial policies which tend to endorse rather than challenge the views of their typical readers.

These and other methodological difficulties are reflected in the marked lack of a consensus in academic opinion. In his impressive historical overview, Franklin (2004: 208–19) identifies four quite distinctive schools of thought on the issue of media effects, beginning in the years before World War II and extending to the present. The first of these emphasised the power of the media, not so much to influence as to control public behaviour. Thereafter, however, research findings have largely moved away from what appears now to be a rather simplistic approach. This began with Lazarsfeld, Berelson and Gaudet's hugely influential *The People's Choice* (1944), which argued that the media affected individual attitudes but only through local 'opinion leaders' who interpreted their messages before passing them on. Later, a third and highly influential view went much further and portrayed media audiences as sovereign consumers who selected media content simply to satisfy their own needs. This model was heavily influenced by the work of psychologists in respect of a theory known as **cognitive dissonance** (see the glossary at the end of this chapter). This 'uses-and-gratifications' model is rightly described by Franklin (2004: 214) as 'a sobering corrective to earlier assertions of media omnipotence'. In terms of political communications, it implies that, at most, the media can do no more than reinforce existing attitudes.

More recently, however, the tide flowing against media influence has ebbed a little. This has given rise to a fourth model, which presents us with a much more complex picture of media–audience interaction. This denies to both parties the capacity to act autonomously. Instead, it suggests that journalists will load onto their content a host of messages, which reflect their personal views together with the dominant news values and a host of structural factors. The extent to which the audience absorbs these preferred meanings will, in turn, depend upon their own values and the social situations which give rise to them. The audience is no more autonomous than the journalist. It may decode the latter's messages in ways which lead to their full and uncritical acceptance; equally, it may not.

Media effects and elections

These broad trends in academic research have shaped the work of political scientists seeking to identify the media's effect on voting behaviour. The significance of their work has been spiced by claims, endorsed by certain politicians, that the media's coverage of politics has proved decisive in determining electoral outcomes. One inevitably thinks of *The Sun*'s bombast in April 1992, when it claimed that John Major owed his victory to the paper's political support.

Election	Party supported by *The Sun*	Conservative share of its readers' vote (%)	Labour share of its readers' vote (%)	Liberal Democrat share of its readers' vote (%)
1992	Conservative	41	31	19
1997	Labour	30	52	12

Table 8.1 A *Sun* effect?

(*Source:* Kettle 2008)

However, it is worth noting that similar claims are still being made. The most recent of these was the suggestion that the *Evening Standard* had helped Boris Johnson win election as London Mayor in 2008 (Jones, Gibson and Brook 2008). It is certainly true that research evidence can be found to support this view. This was especially true of the 1992 general election, where data detected an 8 per cent swing from Labour to the Conservatives among readers of *The Sun* in the seven to eight months before the election (Linton 1995). Similar swings were also evident in other pro-Tory papers but not the anti-Conservative *Guardian*. As Franklin (2004: 219) observes, one has to travel only a very short journey to conclude that the transformation in Labour's political fortunes after 1992 was the direct result of the press's subsequent decision to abandon John Major for Tony Blair.

By and large, however, British political science has been generally sceptical of such claims. This can be explained by the enduring influence of the uses and gratifications model and its idea that voters 'filter' media messages, thereby limiting their impact (Denver 2007: 136). This is evident in the two pioneering studies of the effects of television on voters (Trenaman and McQuail 1961; Blumler and McQuail 1968), both of which concluded that, whilst television was better placed than other media to overcome this 'filter', it did so only in the sense that it was able to increase the amount of information available to voters. Denver (2007: 139) also records that more recent studies, such as those of Miller (1991) and Norris et al. (1999), have been very reluctant to depart significantly from these earlier evaluations.

The so-called 'filter model' seemed particularly relevant to newspapers. Unlike television, the press are free to be partisan in their coverage, something of which readers generally had a clear understanding. The inference drawn by academics was that people, often as a result of family and other person-to-person influences, simply read those newspapers whose editorial policy they found most favourable. At best, a minor reinforcement effect, whereby newspapers strengthened the partisan loyalties of their readers, was measurable. However, there was 'little to support the hypothesis that people switched parties as a result of reading a paper with a particular partisan bias' (Denver 2007: 141). This scepticism is supported by some well-placed insiders. In an interesting contribution to the debate, Kettle (2008) insists that it is the economic imperative which dominates the partisan bias of newspapers. Consequently, Kettle asserts that the principal reason *The Sun* shifted to Labour after 1992 was the need to appease a readership which was already leaving the Conservative party. Hence his warning that 'Politicians who obsess about each day's newspapers are looking in the wrong direction'. They should look to build electoral support first, knowing that newspaper support will invariably follow.

Pause for thought

These conclusions clearly trouble Denver, especially those made in respect of television. In his words, it defies 'common sense to suggest that such a pervasive and powerful medium has little impact on political attitudes and behaviour'. Franklin (2004: 223–4) concurs and argues that the 'learning effect' recorded as early as the 1960s was erroneously underestimated by the original researchers. If television plays a key part in increasing voters' political knowledge, it follows that, in turn, its content 'may subsequently be used by voters when deciding which party to support'. Accordingly, the validity of television research may be questioned on four grounds:

- The scope of many of the original television studies was very narrow.
- These deficiencies have not been properly corrected by any subsequent full-scale studies.

- The very nature of television coverage has changed dramatically during the interim period. It is more extensive, less deferential and infinitely more sophisticated. In addition, television has afforded much more air time to commentators. Their impact – as yet unmeasured in the UK – has been evaluated in the USA. Studies of the aftermath of the 1976 presidential debate between Gerald Ford and Jimmy Carter suggest that the reaction of TV commentators helped swing public opinion behind Carter (Franklin 2004)
- Most importantly, the wider social context in which television operates has changed, particularly partisan dealignment's obvious potential to weaken the filter on media content.

Kuhn (2007: 257) also detects a change in academic opinion and, as the following quotation indicates, strongly supports Denver's contention that the changing socio-political environment in particular has forced researchers to rethink their previous reliance on the uses and gratifications model.

> The possibility that the media may exercise a more important influence than allowed for by the minimal effects model has been boosted over the past quarter century by evidence such as the decline in the mobilisation function of political parties, partisan dealignment among the electorate, electoral volatility and a marked reluctance on the part of some sections of the electorate to vote at all.

In addition, Kuhn extends a media effect to the newspapers. In particular, he sets great store by Newton and Brynin's 2001 research which notes a specific and important effect in which newspaper readership can be linked to voter choice among that increasingly large section of the electorate lacking strong partisan identification. He adds that this reinforces the claims of those such as Linton (1995) who argued that the Conservatives benefited in the 1992 general election from their advantage in newspaper circulation.

It should be added that Kuhn is careful not to overstate the extent of this newspaper effect on voting behaviour. Such revised viewpoints do not dispute the enduring importance of education, gender, class, and so on. What they do argue, especially in the age of dealignment, is that these factors are no longer so overwhelming that they exclude the possibility of a media effect.

Table 8.2 Sources of information during the 2005 general election (figures as percentage of the electorate)

Information source	Respondents who obtained 'a lot' of their information via this source	Respondents who obtained either 'a lot' or 'some' of their information via this source	Respondents who obtained either 'a little' or 'no' information via this source
Television	48.0	72.1	27.5
Newspapers	22.8	48.1	51.4
Radio	10.6	27.4	71.5
Internet	3.3	7.8	90.8
Magazines	1.5	6.8	92.3
Family and friends	5.7	18.8	81
Party literature	17.2	41.3	58.4

(*Source:* Butler and Kavanagh 2006: 169)

In short there is a newspaper effect on voting behaviour. It may be small and variable (e.g. between elections; between party identifiers and non-party identifiers; between broadsheet and tabloid readers), but it is still evident and can in the circumstances of a close electoral contest have significant consequences for the overall result. (Kuhn 2007: 260)

The media and the political agenda

Clearly the scholarly jury is still out on a media effect on voting behaviour and, given the methodological problems inherent in effects-research to which all commentators allude, is likely to remain so for some time yet. Consequently, in this section we move away from this seemingly eternal debate and examine instead the less quantifiable but possibly more rewarding issue of a possible media effect on the conduct of politics *per se*. This will begin by looking at the media's ability to set the political agenda, before going on to explore the media's impact on the behaviour of individual politicians.

> ## Box 8.2 Media influence on the political agenda (selected examples)
>
> ### Media intervention to suppress certain political issues
>
> - 1987: constitutional reform
> - 1992: 'caring issues', especially health care
>
> ### Media intervention to promote their own issues
>
> - 1987: defence
> - 1997: sleaze; UK relations with the European Union
> - 2005: Iraq

Shaping the political agenda

Following Kavanagh's earlier study (Kavanagh 1995), Raymond Kuhn (2007: 245) explains that the political agenda is set as a result of a complex series of interactions between the media, parties and voters. However, he adds that, though it is disputed by some, it is possible within this conceptualisation for journalists to successfully counter the media management strategies of the parties and impose their own ideas on what we should all be discussing. As Box 8.2 suggests, this may involve keeping the parties' preferred items off the agenda, pressing them to discuss items they would prefer to ignore and, most importantly, telling the electorate how it should think. These have invariably worked to the benefit of some parties at the expense of others. In both 1987 and 1992, for example, the main beneficiaries were the Conservatives. Five years later, this situation was reversed with Labour benefiting from the media's determination to focus on issues which reminded the electorate of Tory hypocrisy and internal disunity.

However, once again the idea that there are measurable consequences flowing from the media's influence over the news agenda is disputed by academic observers. This is particularly the case in general election campaigns, where both Miller (1991) and Norris et al. (1999) failed to find any evidence that the news agenda set by the media actually influenced voter attitudes to the salience of political issues. However, as Kuhn (2007: 260) points out, this does not necessarily rule out the possibility of an independent agenda-setting effect over longer-term effect.

Blair and Murdoch

It is possible, however, to argue that the entire debate on media effects rather misses the point. In a very important sense, it is not whether the media can influence the political agenda (and with it voter attitudes) but whether politicians believe that they can. This aspect to the debate on media effects has come into much sharper focus as a result of the relationship between Tony Blair and Rupert Murdoch.

Blair's determination to court the media magnate had been apparent within the first year of his leadership of the Labour party. There were various elements to this, including supporting his private business interests and agenda on media policy (see Chapters 9 and 10) and what Price (2006) calls the 'innumerable "scoops" and favours' given to *The Sun* and *The Times*. However, Price goes on to argue that, during his time as Campbell's deputy, he was aware of a series of ongoing discussions at the very highest levels of government with either Murdoch or one of his deputies. He describes the effect as follows: 'No big decision could ever be made inside No. 10 without taking account of the likely reaction of three men – Gordon Brown, John Prescott and Rupert Murdoch. On all the really big decisions, anybody else could be safely ignored.'

As evidence, Price cites Blair's hesitation over European economic and monetary union, culminating in the decision to abandon a referendum on the euro, and the lurch to the right over immigration and asylum policy. Subsequently and in addition, Geoffrey Wheatcroft (2007) alleges that British policy on Iraq was ultimately shaped by Blair's concern over the likely reaction of Murdoch. The latter was an ardent supporter of the US policy of intervention and Wheatcroft argues that 'a series of telephone calls between Blair and Murdoch just before the invasion of Iraq' proved decisive in firming up British policy.

There will be some for whom the mere image of a UK prime minister discussing the most important foreign policy issue of the time with an Australian newspaper magnate domiciled in the US will be disturbing. However, this does not of course demonstrate a measurable, that is, quantifiable, effect in ways which might satisfy academic researchers. Indeed, Price himself acknowledges this when he states that the impact of Murdoch on specific areas of government policy, especially the extent to which he actually vetoed individual decisions, awaits proper research. Nonetheless, the issues he raises suggest that, depending upon the party, its communications strategy and the context in which the latter is formulated, certain media organisations can acquire the equivalent of Sartori's '**blackmail potential**'. In terms of Blair's relations with Murdoch, the admittedly anecdotal evidence points to a deliberate policy of 'factoring-in' the latter's anticipated reaction on a host of issues where he was known to have a view. This is most definitely not a generalised media effect. Indeed, the same communications strategy effectively guaranteed that other proprietors and their titles would be largely ignored. Rather the point is that Mr Murdoch 'owned newspapers that are bought and read by classic swing voters' (Price 2006), the implication being that the Blair government lacked confidence in its ability to retain the loyalty of these voting groups without his support and reacted accordingly.

Side effects: the media and the crisis of political communications

A third dimension to the debate on media effects is the extent to which the behavior of the media has contributed to 'an ongoing crisis of public communication in Britain' (Kuhn 2007: 263). This critique obviously chimes with the arguments raised by Tony Blair in his June 2007 Lecture on Public Life. Part of the problem is the relentless nature of the media's coverage of politics and politicians. This has served to ratchet up the pressure on politicians to perform perfectly in each media encounter and might explain and possibly even justify the defensive-aggressiveness behind the spinning, monitoring and rebuttal described in Chapters 5 and 6. It might also shed new light on the reasons why the parties have become embroiled in so many funding scandals in their bid to finance a daily campaigning presence.

However, the key element to this debate is the way in which media reporting has corrupted the political process itself. The notion of a dysfunctional journalism is particularly associated with the academics Blumler and Gurevitch (1995), who seek to explain it through five contemporaneous developments.

Box 8.3 Campaign finance

Another notable indirect effect of the media is the growing pressure on parties to raise unprecedented amounts of money to finance their political communications. One consequence of this is that the main parties have to find the means of servicing very large debt. In 2008, the Labour party was rumoured to be as much as £24 million in the red (Hinsliff 2008). A second is the scramble to secure the support of individual financial backers, exposing the parties to allegations of corruption. This began under the premiership of John Major (Foster 1994) and continued throughout the Blair years, culminating in the remarkable police investigation into the so-called 'cash-for-honours' affair.

Nor did the scandals stop with Blair's resignation. By the end of November 2007, the main opposition parties were demanding that the police investigate donations worth as much as £600,000 allegedly channelled into Labour coffers by north-east property developer David Abrahams. Concern focused on Abrahams' use of third parties to disguise his financial contributions, which appeared to be all the more disturbing in light of government intervention to allow Abrahams to go ahead with the construction of a business park in Co. Durham after planning permission had been originally denied (*Guardian*, 29 November 2007). The Abrahams affair rumbled on throughout 2008 and led to the resignation of at least one key Labour official. Indeed, it was a measure of Labour's concern that it attempted to turn media attention towards alleged Conservative peccadilloes, namely the tax status of their leading financial backer and tax exile Lord Ashcroft (Woodward 2008) and the alleged failure of shadow chancellor George Osborne to reveal the names of the five donors who financed his private office (Hencke 2008).

The first of these refers generally to the way in which politics tends to be reported. There is an important technical context here. News production has been revolutionised by the advent of electronic news gathering (ENG). This has dramatically increased the speed at which news is collated and inserted into news broadcasts. Precisely because they can process the news far more quickly, editors can increase the number of items covered. In turn, this reduces the amount of time they allocate to each campaign item. This trend was first visible in the US, where analysis suggested that the time available to the presidential candidates to deliver their sound bites fell from 42 seconds in 1968 to eight in 1996 (Jones 2006: 224). British broadcasters have duly followed suit, leaving politicians with a clear sense that more is less.

The second aspect of this trend is the increase in 'process' and 'horse-race' journalism. This refers to the tendency of media organisations to report politics in part as soap opera, in part as sporting contest. The effect is what Lloyd (2004: 195) calls the 'privileging of conflict and complaint'. This acts both to dramatise otherwise mundane intra-party disagreements and ensures that evidence of policy success is rarely, if ever, reported. For Blumler and Gurevitch, the effect of the above, which utterly distorts public perceptions of the political process, is compounded by a third development: the manner in which the character of political journalism has changed. Essentially, journalism in Britain has reconfigured itself over the last three decades to assume the role of the real opposition to the 'political class'. This theme figures prominently in John Lloyd's famous polemic on deteriorating journalistic standards (Lloyd 2004). According to another insider account (Oborne and Walters 2004) it can be also given a sociological construct in the form of a new generation of journalists – the new media class – whose attitude to politicians is the very opposite of deferential. The result is a marked tendency for journalists to view themselves less as reporters and much more as critics with the moral authority to challenge and indeed condemn politicians. This has given rise to numerous consequences:

- Firstly, there is the phenomenon of strategic framing or what Kuhn (2007: 264) calls the 'glut of interpretative journalism'. This means that news items are rarely reported without a commentary, which explains to the audience what it is the politician is really trying to tell them. Politicians and their media managers find this immensely frustrating. Aside from the valuable space and especially time it takes up, strategic framing acts as yet another filter through which their messages have to pass before they can reach the electorate.

- However, from our immediate perspective it is the sub-text of strategic framing that is particularly important. As Lloyd (2004: 159) notes, the implication is quite clear: all official briefings can be dismissed as 'spin', the conduct of politicians being so inherently untrustworthy that only journalistic commentary can prevent the public from being duped.

- The hyper-adversarialism of the new media class has also encouraged journalists to condemn politicians in highly personalised attacks. The most dramatic manifestation of this tendency is 'attack journalism', which has seen off the careers of numerous ministers and gave rise to Tony Blair's descriptor of contemporary journalists as a 'feral pack'.

The media's obsession with the personal failings of politicians also points to a fourth and more worrying feature of contemporary journalism. It suggests that the hounding of ministers who appear to have fallen from grace is neither mere opportunism nor the product of lazy journalism but central to what it is the news media are there to do: entertain. This has debased news coverage, not only by reprioritising the value of news stories in ways which afford primacy to the personal and trivial (Kuhn 2007: 263), but also in neglecting entire classes of news item, most notably foreign affairs, which should demand inclusion. Franklin (1997) famously coined the term 'newszak' to describe this process. In the age of 'infotainment' journalists take care to make as few demands as possible on their audiences.

The impact of 'newszak' is compounded by Blumler and Gurevitch's final criticism. This argues that journalists *per se* are increasingly inclined to use the same overarching frame to report on politics, one in which the public is presented with a dominant image of itself as cynical and disillusioned. This can easily become a self-fulfilling prophecy, the high levels of voter absenteeism in recent general elections being the most obvious evidence of this. Polly Toynbee – one of Britain's leading newspaper columnists – agrees. She has argued, consistently and with some passion, that news reporting in the UK is dominated by three core values, all of them highly negative: generating (often false) fear; showing that nothing government does ever works; and convincing voters that, no matter what is attempted, everything will get worse. The combined effect, as per Blair's critique, is to encourage an automatic, unthinking distrust of politicians and public officials to a degree whereby 'The media is in danger of making government by any party impossible'. Toynbee

Box 8.4 Criteria of newsworthiness

- Timing and frequency
- Amplitude
- Anticipation
- Surprise
- Response of other media organisations
- Relation to other news items
- Reference to elites
- Personalisation
- Negativity

(*Source:* Negrine 1994: 120–3)

concludes her coruscating attack by pointing to two additional characteristics of journalism which, if anything, are even worse. One: a complete absence of self-awareness; two: naked hypocrisy. Consequently, she notes that media business is 'done with corrupting cheque book, threat, intimidation, invasion of privacy, paparazzi aggression and vicious cruelty' (2007), all far, far more damaging than the conduct of the politicians they so routinely condemn.

Final effects: the media and political society

The notions of 'dumbing down' and 'infotainment' are particularly pertinent to the fourth dimension to the debate on media effects. This refers us to what Curran and Seaton (2003: 322) call the 'sociology of the mass media' and, in particular, the work of a hugely distinguished group of critical theorists known as the Frankfurt School.

The initial impetus behind the work of these scholars was to explain the rise of fascism and Nazism, something which led them inevitably to consider the role of the media in creating a 'mindset' conducive to ultra-right-wing dictatorships. However, it was only when they settled in the US as political exiles that their ideas on a media effect began to crystallise into an overarching critique. The catalyst was their exposure to the mass culture rapidly developing on US radio, in its cinemas and, later, in television broadcasts. For the

Frankfurt School, not only was this inferior to the older European cultures it was driving out, but by generating a culture of passivity it was encouraging the very personality traits which lead directly to subservience in the face of right-wing demagogues. What followed was (and still is!) a stimulating and challenging critique of middle-class culture, the retreat into isolated private life which is so marked in advanced capitalist society and the emergence of a socio-cultural vacuum filled by the mass media. It concludes with the idea that the media in western societies has created a culture which is standardised, vulgar and of ersatz inferiority; one in which every aspect of our lives is subjugated to commercial values. Once again, at the heart of this horribly bleak description is the media's sole dynamic: to entertain. The effect, according to the Frankfurt School, is akin to the administration of a narcotic, in which individuals come to desire 'false wants' at the expense of the development of their real and unique personalities. In response to the assertion that in consuming the products of the mass media, people are seeking harmless escape from an otherwise mundane and unglamorous life, the Frankfurt scholars counter by arguing that, on the contrary, the mass media is actually imprisoning people in such a life through promoting a value system which reduces all human needs to material consumption and social activity to the means of acquiring the financial means of doing so.

One of the key limitations of studies of this type is that they draw their readers' attention to ideas they lack the space to develop. Nowhere is this problem more striking than in respect of the Frankfurt School. The latter encapsulates in an imaginative albeit complex way Marx's original critique of the bourgeoisie as a once-revolutionary class which has lost its ability to recreate itself as a positive historical force, with his twentieth-century followers' concern that bourgeois capitalism had, nonetheless, found ways of protecting itself through the corruption of the working class. As Curran and Seaton (2003: 328) observe: 'As a consequence, the Frankfurt School saw the function of the media, whether in the long run or more directly, as controlling the public in the interests of Capital'.

It is stating the case mildly to say that such a view is highly contentious, though this should make it more, not less, worthy of study. However, from our immediate perspective, it suggests that the most powerful if the least quantifiable of all the media effects we have examined is to reproduce an entire economic and political system, one which all good Marxists (and quite a few bad ones) might argue would have otherwise succumbed to its own internal contradictions and collapsed long ago.

Conclusion

This chapter has aimed to show something of the breadth of the academic and political debate on media effects. It began with the possibility of a media effect on elections and proceeded through the media's ability to set the political agenda before concluding with an assessment of several arguments that the media might have corrupted not only the political process, but also society itself. If nothing else, this ought to show that the study of contemporary politics is impossible without reference to a media effect of some sort. This being so, one might wonder whether the parties of government have been motivated to intervene in this process, either to limit the effect of the media or channel it to their political advantage. To answer this question, we must now turn to the issue of media policy.

. . . .

 What you should have gained from reading this chapter

- Insight into academic theories on generalised media effects.

- An appreciation of the ongoing controversy over the media's effect on voting behaviour.

- An understanding of some of the different ways in which commentators conceptualise media effects.

- Why it is argued that the media has contributed to a crisis in political communication.

- An idea of the main arguments of the Frankfurt School.

 Glossary of key terms

Blackmail potential A concept associated with the work of political scientist Giovanni Sartori, which suggests that the mere presence of a party at key points on the ideological spectrum can change the policy positions of other parties, including the party of government.

Cognitive dissonance This suggests that the media audience will subconsciously avoid content which challenges its deepest beliefs and values. Faced with hostile information or viewpoints, the mind intervenes to prevent unnecessary distress and 'filters' media content to remove these harmful items.

Couch potato An abusive term ridiculing the tendency of some individuals to sit at home, living their lives through television programmes. Popular TV characters such as Homer Simpson and Jim Royle personify such people.

Psephologists Those who study voting behaviour, a term derived from the Greek 'psephos', meaning pebble.

Likely examination questions

Why has the debate on a media effect on voting behaviour proved so inconclusive?

What does it mean to say that the media has an effect on the political agenda?

In what ways has the media contributed to a crisis in politics and political communication?

Helpful websites

As in so many aspects of media politics, the *Guardian* newspaper's media section is an invaluable source of information and can be found at www.guardian.co.uk/media. *The Independent*'s media section is located at www.independent.co.uk/media.

Further reading

As with the debate on media bias, the possibility of a media effect is discussed in a number of the leading textbooks. The reader's attention is drawn to Chapter 4 of Street's *Mass Media, Politics and Democracy*, Chapter 10 of Raymond Kuhn's *Politics*, Chapter 9 of Bob Franklin's *Packaging Politics* and Chapter 5 of Brian McNair's *An Introduction to Political Communication*. Chapter 6 of David Denver's *Elections and Voters in Britain* (Basingstoke: Palgrave Macmillan, 2007) places the relationship between the media and voting behaviour in its proper psephological context. Finally, Chapter 20 of Curran and Seaton's *Power Without Responsibility* offers an excellent introduction to the work of the Frankfurt School.

Media Policy (1): Ownership

Contents

Overview

The twin debates on media bias and effects throw into sharper relief the outline of government media policy. Put simply: if the media are biased and, further, that this could have a significant effect on political outcomes, it follows that government has a powerful incentive to control their behaviour through public policy. We have already acquired some insight into this in Chapter 6, when we saw how ministers can use the law to censor the media. Now we have to examine the extent to which politicians have taken this approach a stage further by regulating who can own media organisations.

Key issues to be covered in this chapter

- Theoretical approaches to media ownership
- Patterns of ownership in the print and broadcast media
- The growth of sectoral concentration and the loss of diversity within the print media
- The consequences of the rise of cross-media ownership
- The demands for changes to government policy in order to preserve both pluralism and diversity within the media

Media ownership in perspective

Though the presence of three public broadcast corporations hints at something of a 'mixed economy', the overwhelming majority of media organisations in the UK remain in private hands. This does not of itself exclude the possibility of state intervention. Indeed, as the list below indicates, government has numerous ways to influence media markets whilst continuing to allow most outlets to remain in private hands:

- Ownership may be licensed in order to disbar certain individuals or corporate interests from acquiring media organisations.
- Ownership within each media sector (newspapers, radio, television, etc.) might be restricted to a specific number of outlets or a maximum share of the market.
- Similarly, the ability of individuals to acquire outlets across different media sectors (what is known as cross-media diversification) might be heavily constrained, or even outlawed altogether.
- Government may also choose to provide some media services directly through publicly owned organisations or indirectly by subsidising their privately owned equivalents.

Running though these – and similar – issues are two broad and competing perspectives on the media. The first emphasises the media as a form of economic activity. An excellent example of the latter is the Labour government's 2000 White Paper 'A New Future for Communications'. It follows that any attempt to regulate ownership must take into account economic realities. However, what one might call the neo-liberal perspective also argues that, by allowing market forces to determine patterns of ownership, policy-makers will also ensure the best possible outcome for the consumers of media output.

This, it must be added, is a highly contentious point and is vehemently opposed by those who favour a **dirigiste** approach. They reject the primacy of the economic model along with any suggestion that it can meet the needs of democratic politics. The case for intervention asserts that, without an expansive media policy, a privately owned media market will consistently fail. This is the basis of the public service model of broadcasting, which has proved so influential in shaping broadcasting policy in Britain since the 1920s. However,

Table 9.1 National newspaper circulation: February 2007–February 2009

	February 2007	February 2008	February 2009	% change
Sun	3,072,392	3,077,060	2,954,298	-3.84
Daily Mirror	1,564,082	1,500,543	1,326,628	-15.2
Daily Star	779,023	723,905	780,742	+0.19
Daily Record	412,844	394,1879	349,127	-15.4
Daily Mail	2,339,733	2,294,880	2,218,547	-5.18
Daily Express	761,637	736,634	715,280	-6.09
Daily Telegraph	896,476	866,693	821,943	-8.31
Times	642,711	613,068	607,775	-5.44
Financial Times	445,276	448,342	421,026	-5.44
Guardian	364,491	355,634	340,238	-6.65
Independent	264,182	252,435	205,964	-22.0
News of the World	3,371,369	3,281,287	3,019,928	-10.4
Sunday Mirror	1,374,786	1,348,395	1,226,062	-10.8
People	746,083	653,909	585,527	-21.5
Sunday Mail	508,594	484,331	438,637	-13.8
Daily Star Sunday	384,060	336,523	360,143	-6.3
Mail on Sunday	2,263,980	2,203,642	2,184,982	-3.5
Sunday Express	816,351	676,165	635,846	-22.1
Sunday Times	1,245,483	1,206,247	1,214,254	-2.5
Sunday Telegraph	667,692	633,193	595,029	-10.9
Observer	442,137	464,005	430,341	-2.7
Independent on Sunday	239,585	228,012	179,487	-25.1

(Source: Audit Bureau of Circulation)

more radical critics would like to see this approach extended to ownership of the print media. This is especially so where, as we saw in the previous chapter, it is argued that the latter play a key part in preserving the social status quo and the principle of capitalist property relations on which it is based.

Government policy on newspaper ownership

Since the middle of the nineteenth century, government policy towards newspaper ownership has consistently rejected intervention. Matters had not always been this way. For nearly two centuries the press had been subject to various forms of licensing. In their final manifestation, licensed publishers had to pay a variety of duties, which had a significant impact on their costs. Today, the cover price of a 'quality' newspaper is in the region of 90 pence. If the duties levied two centuries ago were re-imposed, this would rise to well over £3. In this way, licensing acted to restrict newspaper purchasing to the well-to-do, thereby removing any economic incentive to publish titles which might appeal to the tastes and more importantly the political interests of the lower orders.

The licensing system was finally dismantled between 1853 and 1861. Whilst the extent to which this was truly a liberalising measure is open to debate (Curran and Seaton 2003), its historical impact is beyond dispute. On the one hand, anyone is free to enter the market. On the other, thanks to the process of industrialisation described below, entry is in reality restricted to those with access to seemingly unlimited amounts of capital. The fact that government has consistently rejected subsidising certain newspapers in the wider public interest has made ownership essentially 'a rich man's game'. This does not mean that government has abandoned the notion of market regulation altogether. A regulatory regime of sorts was eventually put in place in the years after World War II (see Box 9.1), a recognition that newspapers enjoy a special status and are not to be treated in the same way as all other businesses. Yet it constitutes regulation of the lightest possible touch. In particular, the system has always ensured that ministers have the decisive say and, as the following list should show, rarely have the latter been overly inclined to use their powers in ways which undermine the interests of the leading players.

Box 9.1 The regulation of newspaper ownership

The 'old regime': the Fair Trading Act 1973
Throughout the twentieth century ministers have largely depended upon competition legislation to protect consumers against the emergence of newspaper monopolies. However, between 1965 and 2002 additional provisions also applied. These were eventually consolidated in ss. 57–62 of the Fair Trading Act 1973 and obliged ministers to personally approve any acquisition which resulted in the proprietor enjoying a combined circulation in excess of 500,000. Further, before granting approval ministers were required to refer the proposed sale to the Competition Commission. In essence, these provisions enabled the authorities to block the acquisition of newspaper titles on public interest as well as competition grounds. For example, in May 1990 the sale of two regional newspapers to *Daily Sport* owner David Sullivan was blocked owing to fears that the accurate presentation of the news and the standing of the newspapers would be compromised (Robertson and Nicol 2008: 742–3).

The new regime: the amended Enterprise Act 2002
In 2002, Labour replaced the previous regime with the Enterprise Act 2002. This was highly controversial in that it removed the public interest justification for intervention. This was the Blair government at its most neo-liberal, a stance which provoked considerable criticisms along with the usual batch of accusations that the government was producing policy designed to appeal to the business interests of the leading newspaper proprietors. One year later, during the passage of the 2003 Communications Act, Labour relented and reinstated the public interest provisions, albeit in much modified form. These are now known as 'special public interest considerations' and include such items as 'the need for the accurate presentation of news and free expression of opinion in newspapers and the need (*so far as this is reasonable and practicable*) for a sufficient plurality of views in newspapers in the relevant market' (Robertson and Nicol 2008: 741).

- Firstly, both ministers and the competition authorities have a remarkable record of allowing new owners to acquire titles without let or hindrance. Of the 191 applications they considered between November 1973 and December 2003, only 10 (or 5.2 per cent) were refused or granted subject to conditions.

Box 9.2 The industrialisation of the press

This process began in the immediate aftermath of the collapse of press licensing. From a contemporary perspective, its most striking feature was the emergence of a number of titles which have survived to the present: the *Daily Telegraph* (founded in 1855), *The People* (1881), the *Daily Mail* (1896), the *Daily Express* (1900) and the *Daily Mirror* (1903). The owners of these new titles quickly recognised that economics of newspaper production had changed radically and that the survival of their titles depended on their ability to secure advertising revenue. By the end of the nineteenth century, advertising agencies had acquired large budgets. The £20 million they had at their disposal in 1907 rose to £59 million three decades later; a phenomenal amount of money which, in the absence of commercial broadcasting, was largely spent via newspapers and magazines. To attract advertising revenue, newspapers needed to boost sales. The most effective way to do this was simply to slash cover prices and expand editorial and promotional budgets exponentially. Unfortunately, relatively few media organisations had the capital to do this. At a time of rapidly rising production costs, those who could not attract advertising revenue simply went bust.

- Secondly, ministers have consistently used loopholes in the law to avoid referring certain applications to the competition authorities in the first place. This is especially so when they have been faced with potentially damaging clashes with the leading proprietors. Two particularly notable examples are the Conservatives' refusal to intervene in Rupert Murdoch's purchase of *The Times* and *Sunday Times* in 1981 and Labour's failure to refer Richard Desmond's purchase of the Express Group in November 2000.

- Thirdly, ministers have never used anti-competition law to prevent the more aggressive owners deliberately cutting their cover prices in order to undermine their rivals. Tony Blair's government even went so far as to overrule the House of Lords and keep such a measure out of the 2002 Enterprise Act.

- Further, and most importantly, governments have consistently resisted the pressure to place statutory restrictions on the number of titles owned by an individual organisation or a ceiling on its market share. Multiple ownership has been commonplace for

Table 9.2 The decline of newspaper titles: 1921–2002

Category	1921	2002	Net % reduction
National daily	14	12	14.3
National Sunday	14	11	21.4
Regional morning	41	19	53.6
Regional evening	93	74	20.4

years, with the current market leader – Rupert Murdoch's News International – owing four national titles.

- Finally, it is axiomatic that governments have never used public funds to underpin plurality of ownership and supply. Whenever newspapers have found themselves in financial difficulties, they have either closed or been absorbed into larger media group.

Trends in newspaper ownership: sectoral concentration and the loss of diversity

The *laissez-faire* attitudes of British government towards newspaper ownership have become more significant in light of the ongoing changes to the market conditions in which the print media operate. In the decades which followed the industrialisation of the press, an expanding newspaper industry rapidly attracted new capital, a new type of owner and, most importantly, a new economic rationale (see Box 9.2 above).

As the twentieth century wore on, the importance of capitalisation increased still further as circulation went into decline and the market became ever more competitive. In 1950, for example, the total circulation enjoyed by the national daily press was 16,632,000. However, within two decades this figure had fallen below 15 million and has continued to decline ever since. One can gain a sense of this from the data listed in Table 9.1. By the summer of 2009, the national dailies were selling fewer than 11 million copies. Even then, this figure was achieved because of price-cutting and the sale of '**bulks**'. Nor is there any sign that this trend will be reversed. At the time of writing

Table 9.3 Declining circulation in the Scottish press (March 2009)

Title	Circulation	Year-on-year decline (%)
Herald	59,546	-10.7
Scotsman	49,113	-7.56
Daily Record	358,290	-8.55
Sunday Mail	443,242	-8.46
Sunday Post	361,371	-9.69
Scotland on Sunday	63,166	-11.81
Sunday Herald	41,046	-17.7

(*Source:* Sheerin 2009)

it was rumoured that the owners of the two *Independent* titles and *The Observer* were looking to sell them on.

The first consequence of this has been a constant reduction in the number of individual titles. Despite the fact that attention invariably focuses on the national picture, it is clearly the regional press which has taken the biggest 'hit' in terms of declining titles. The decline in levels of choice has been particularly stark. For example, in 1921 readerships in no fewer than 15 urban centres had a choice of a regional morning paper. By 2002, that figure had declined to a mere two. In the regional evening markets the decline in choice was even starker, the corresponding figures being 27 and zero (all data Curran and Seaton 2003: 351–2).

The decline of the regional press has been felt particularly acutely in Scotland. Here, the circulation figures of the Scotland-wide titles have continued to suffer as more and more Scottish readers prefer the Scottish editions of the leading London-based titles, whose competitive pricing and promotional budgets make for a much more attractive product. The Scottish Affairs Committee has been sufficiently alarmed by this to publish figures which suggest that half of the 1,500 or so titles in Scotland will have been closed by 2014, a

Table 9.4 The leading newspaper groups in the UK

Group	Average weekly circulation	Titles	Share of national market (%)
News International	7,847,741	The Sun, The Times, News of the World, Sunday Times	36.3
Daily Mail and General	4,260,205	Daily Mail, Mail on Sunday	19.7
Trinity Mirror	3,925,051	Mirror, Daily Record, Sunday Mirror, People, Sunday Mail	18.1
Northern and Shell	2,625,560	Daily Express, Daily Star, Sunday Express, Daily Star on Sunday	12.1
Telegraph Media Group	1,454,754	Daily Telegraph, Sunday Telegraph	6.72
Scott Trust	746,004	The Guardian, The Observer	3.45
Financial Times Groups (UK)	411,906	Financial Times	1.90
Independent News and Media	362,873	The Independent, Independent on Sunday	1.68

gloomy prediction but one which is perfectly consistent with trends across other regions.

The loss in the number of titles has led inexorably to another trend: the concentration of the surviving titles into increasingly powerful newspaper groups (Table 9.4). The result is that 'Britain has one of the most concentrated newspaper ownership arrangements in the Western World' (Robertson and Nicol 2007: 740). The four leading groups enjoy 86.2 per cent of national sales, whilst News International alone sells nearly four in every ten newspapers purchased in the UK at that level. In a sign of the increasing integration of the global media market, it is significant that a number of these are under owners, some of them foreign, with extensive interests elsewhere within the media. This is famously so in the case of News International. However, the Daily Mail and General, Trinity Mirror, Northern and Shell and Independent News and Media have large media investments not simply in the UK and Ireland but across the globe.

The loss of diversity
The concentration of ownership has, in turn, led to fears of a loss in diversity. The first sign of this was the decline in the party organ. Though it might surprise the modern reader, there was a time when titles owned by the supporters of a particular party and run in its interest were key features of Britain's newspaper industry. Curran and Seaton (2003: 45) note that at the turn of the century a majority of the London-based press was owned by 'wealthy individuals, families or syndicates closely linked to a political party'. The Conservative party was particularly active, helping to finance the purchase of four major titles immediately prior to World War I and a fifth – the *Morning Post* – in 1924. The Liberals arranged for the purchase of the *Daily News* (1901) and the *Daily Chronicle* (1918), whilst the TUC took over the *Daily Herald* in 1922.

However, such 'wheeling and dealing' merely hid an uncomfortable truth. By the end of the 1920s it was becoming increasingly obvious that only those titles with large editorial and promotional budgets were likely to prosper. The 'political' titles had neither and were soon on the defensive. The first indication of this came in 1926, when the Conservative party was unable to find a backer to prevent the closure of the *Daily Graphic*. Two years later, the various Liberal factions lost both the *Westminster Gazette* and the *Daily Chronicle*. One year later still, the TUC was forced to surrender financial control of the *Daily Herald*. A small number of political titles struggled on until the 1960s, when the death knell finally sounded. First, the great Liberal daily, the *News Chronicle*, was closed down and absorbed into the right-wing Associated Group in October 1960. Later in the

Box 9.3 The fate of the News on Sunday

This title was launched in April 1987. The idea originated with the **Big Flame** group which felt that such a paper was viable with a circulation of 800,000. Within eight weeks, however, circulation had fallen from an initial 500,000 to 200,000 and bankruptcy was avoided only by the intervention of the Transport and General Workers Union. Shortly after the 1987 general election, the paper was sold to Lancashire businessman Owen Oyston. After failing to improve its market position, Oyston closed it for good in November.

The paper failed for two reasons. Firstly, its high-brow, politics-orientated editorial policy deterred working-class readers, who preferred their more traditional Sunday fare of scandal, sensationalism and sport. Secondly, it lacked the finances to break out of this impasse. The News on Sunday needed an extensive budget to promote the paper and survive the inevitable losses until its promotional campaign began to pay off. Without these, it was doomed.

decade and in a sign of things to come, the left-wing *Daily Herald* (renamed *The Sun* in 1964) was sold to a young Australian entrepreneur, Rupert Murdoch, who relaunched it as a tabloid in November 1969.

There is also a strong spatial element to the loss of diversity. This was the theme of a recent **Westminster Hall** debate organised by MPs concerned about the consequences of declining circulation and lost advertising revenue among local newspapers. However, in terms of diversity of content arguably the most important victim has been the radical press. From being a major force in regional and local newspaper markets throughout the nineteenth century, the radical press has declined to the very margins of today's print media. Lacking the capital to compete with the editorial and marketing budgets of the new generation of mass-market papers, one by one these papers either went bust or changed their editorial stance to boost circulation. Though the trade union movement tried periodically to re-establish a mass-circulation radical paper, the last attempt to do so – the *News on Sunday* – ended in embarrassing failure.

The irresistible rise of cross-media ownership

The willingness of British governments to tolerate sectoral concentration is also reflected in changing attitudes towards cross-media ownership. To understand this point, we must first briefly examine the history of British broadcasting. At first, this appears to offer a marked contrast to policy on newspaper ownership. Anxious to avoid a situation where a new and powerful medium might fall into the hands of demagogues, government in the 1920s opted for a state-owned broadcasting monopoly. After protracted discussions on how to protect it from political interference, the BBC was established as a public corporation under Royal Charter on 20 December 1926.

The BBC retained its monopoly on broadcasting until the Television Act 1954 set up Independent Television, financed from the sale of advertising space during broadcast schedules. However, the arrival of commercial television did not lead to a scramble to open new stations. Instead, the number of television companies was tightly controlled by a statutory licensing system. In addition, from 1963 the rules on cross-media ownership were clarified so that strict limits were placed on the ability of newspaper owners to acquire any of these licenses.

By the 1980s, however, the licensing system was coming under extraordinary pressure, largely because the impending arrival of digital broadcasting undermined the chief technical justification for maintenance of the status quo: spectrum scarcity. Demands for reform met with a favourable response from the Thatcher government, which, from 1986 onwards, began to prepare the way for a

---

Box 9.4 The BBC's Charter and Framework Agreement

Since first being issued in 1926, the BBC's Charter has been renewed on numerous occasions; the current version came fully into force on 1 January 2007 and will expire on 31 December 2016. The Charter effectively sets down the BBC's duties. A key role is played by the governors (now members of the BBC Trust) who are under a duty to ensure that the Corporation fulfils its obligations under Articles 4–5 and to protect the interests of licence-fee payers.

radical overhaul of the licensing system. In a speech to the Press Association in June 1989 Thatcher made no secret of her belief that the long-term health of British broadcasting depended upon the arrival of new entrants. This would be especially so in the new digital broadcast markets and would include newspaper companies. The subsequent changes to the law – key statutes were passed in 1990, 1996 and 2003 – are set out in Box 9.5 below.

Box 9.5 The deregulation of broadcasting

Broadcasting Act 1990
This piece of legislation marked the start of a new era in British broadcasting, one in which government has allowed market forces far greater influence. Its main points are set out below:

- The 16 ITV franchises were put up for sale. Four existing companies lost out as a consequence of this: TV-AM, Thames, TVS and TSW.
- The national networking system for ITV was replaced with a more flexible scheme to benefit small franchises and independents.
- The ownership of Independent Television News was broken up.
- Channel 4 was given the power to sell its own advertising .
- A new commercial franchise – Channel 5 – was awarded.
- All television companies, including the BBC, were compelled to buy at least 20 per cent of their programmes from independents .
- Newspaper companies were allowed to acquire cable and satellite licences, though newspapers were still limited to owning no more than a 20 per cent stake of one licence within each category of national radio, television and *domestic* satellite broadcasting.
- The major change in respect of cross-media diversification, however, concerned the reclassification of BSkyB as a foreign satellite broadcaster, thereby enabling Rupert Murdoch to retain ownership of his News International stable of newspapers.

Broadcasting Act 1996
The 1990 Act had destabilised ITV, which, along with a number of newspaper organisations alarmed at News International's privileged position, began to lobby intensively for a relaxation on the rules on internal takeovers. The Major government duly obliged and took the opportunity to further weaken the rules on cross-media ownership:

- With the exception of the London franchises, the rules restricting the number of licences which any broadcaster might own simultaneously were abolished and replaced with a new rule which enabled a broadcaster to own any number of licences up to 15 per cent of the total television audience.
- The rules restricting ownership across the three broadcasting sectors were abolished altogether.
- The rules governing cross-media diversification were considerably liberalised. The 20-per-cent rule was effectively abolished. Only those newspaper groups with a market share of 20 per cent or more were prevented from acquiring a national or regional TV licence. This penalised News International and Trinity Mirror but benefited the other leading newspaper groups.

Communications Act 2003

New Labour policy was initially concerned with shoring up the financial position of ITV by allowing the latter to become a single company in 2001 with a new logo, ITV1. Thereafter, it extended the process of liberalisation still further with new legislation in 2003. Among other things this created a new framework for issuing broadcast licences, including two new and all-important criteria: that a wide variety of programmes should be broadcast; and that new licences should be granted to promote the innovation and competition which ministers insisted was essential for enhanced consumer choice. Though it retained some controls on cross-media ownership, this framework constitutes something of a bare minimum necessary to prevent the emergence of a de facto free market in the commercial broadcast sector.

- The remaining ban on newspapers owning commercial broadcasters was removed.
- The exception to this was a specific provision restricting those newspaper organisations with a 20 per cent market share from owning more than 20 per cent of a national or regional ITV franchise.
- Foreign companies were permitted to own commercial broadcasters.

Three trends are at work here. The first is the way in which in the regulations governing ITV were relaxed to allow more and more licence holders to merge with each other. The second and more important trend has been to allow foreign companies to acquire a stake in British free-to-air broadcasters, 'Five' being owned by the

> ## Box 9.6 The structure of television broadcasting in the UK
>
> Once analogue services are finally switched off, television in Britain will be divided into two broad groups. The first of these is classified as *digital terrestrial television*, or the *'freeview' channels*. This currently consists of nearly 100 channels, including the most popular and well-known on British television. The BBC has applied for and been granted a number of channels, including a 24-hour news channel. Similarly, ITV has also sought to create its own 'family' of channels.
>
> The second group consists of the *digital cable and satellite channels*. There are over 800 of these, the most well known and commercially successful being those broadcast by BSkyB. These can be accessed in various ways, typically via digital cable or satellite-receiving equipment. The key difference between this group and the 'freeview' channels lies in the latter's title: accessing them depends upon taking out a subscription or making some other form of financial payment.

German broadcaster RTL. The third, and from our particular perspective the most important, is the way in which the rules on cross-media diversification have been relaxed to allow newspaper interests to move into the broadcasting market. This process highlights the spread of neo-liberal ideas from the print media to broadcasting. For the most part, only two factors now prevent the emergence of a full and unrestrained market in broadcasting:

- The existence of the BBC and to a lesser extent Channel 4 and S4C as public corporations, though the parlous state of Channel 4's finances are such that, unless the broadcaster receives a considerable injection of government cash, a forced sale to a private-sector buyer will be inevitable.
- The inability of any of the leading newspaper groups to own more than 20 per cent of ITV.

The net effect is that whilst Rupert Murdoch was effectively banned from owning ITV he could theoretically take over ownership of Five. In this way, the Labour government was able to reaffirm its earlier pledge to maintain at least four different free-to-air terrestrial broadcasters.

Ownership: why it matters

Government policy has been widely criticised by those, especially on the political Left, who favour rules restricting ownership. These take two broad forms. The first of these rejects the economic case that technological change effectively guarantees plurality of supply and diversity of content. Instead, it suggests that government policy on ownership has simply invited uncompetitive practices (such as mergers and predatory pricing), with the result that smaller companies have been driven out of the market. The result is widespread market failure, in which commercial values have come to dominate media output across all sectors with all that this implies for the range and diversity of content.

However, it is the second set of arguments – the political – which are the more significant. The first and most important of these is that, by allowing ownership to become so highly concentrated, ministers have handed to individual proprietors extraordinary political influence. This is most obviously so in respect of media policy itself, a point which we have seen in the preceding text and shall revisit in the following chapter. In addition, as we saw in Chapter 8, it can be argued that the dominant proprietors have been able to shape government policy across a wide range of other issues. This is compounded by the fact that, as Stanley Baldwin famously stated, such men (there are very few women) can intervene in politics without ever being called to account for their conduct. Further, the political case for reform insists that concentration of ownership undermines the role that the media should play in strengthening liberal democracy. In summary, it must:

- Act as the mouthpiece for a wide and diverse range of viewpoints
- Stimulate debate
- Encourage dissenting and minority opinion.

The concentration of ownership has the potential to undermine the media on all three points. This is not to say that it will always work to this effect, a point amplified at some length by Street (2001). However, it is undeniably the case that the risk is significant. This was recognised by as conservative a body as the first post-war royal commission on the press: the Ross Commission. Though Ross's words were directed solely at newspapers, their wider application should be obvious. When describing the adverse effects of concentration of ownership he argued that:

> . . . first, that there may be insufficient channels for the expression of opinion and, second, that it may become possible for a very few men to influence the outlook and opinions of large numbers of people by selecting and presenting news in such way as to project a particular view of the world or to support a particular policy (quoted in Kuhn 2007: 107).

Finally, it is the ability of such all-powerful owners to act as 'cultural gatekeeper' (Freedman 2008: 106) which is in many respects the greatest single concern. This returns us to the ideas of the Frankfurt School with all that these imply for the waning capacity of late capitalist societies to resist the forces of illiberalism and authoritarianism.

Explaining government policy

This critique inevitably invites accusations that ministers have, one, capitulated to the interests of big business for fear of alienating the major owners and, two, sought to take political advantage from the culture of passivity and conformity identified by the Frankfurt School. However, whilst it is axiomatic that government policy bears testimony to the enduring influence of neo-liberal ideas, suffice to say that ministers have consistently rejected any accusations that their policy constitutes mere capitulation to big business. Instead, they argue that the rules regulating ownership in Britain simply recognise global economic realities. These mean that, in order both to survive and prosper as important revenue earners, British media companies have to be sufficiently large and powerful to compete in global media markets. This also explains why governments have accepted that leading newspaper organizations will continue to prove much sought-after business partners, especially among commercial broadcasters.

More importantly, the official view also rejects claims that diversity of content depends upon plurality of supply, that is, a large number of media organisations operating in each market. Ministers have pointed out that only the large companies have the capital to print or broadcast a range of content. Given the intensity of market competition, small companies will be drawn inevitably to providing more or less exclusively for the mass entertainment market. Far from increasing diversity, the effect of ownership regulations could be the very opposite: a limited diet aimed solely at boosting circulation and ratings and securing advertising revenue.

This problem highlights some of the major deficiencies in the case for reform. Ultimately, statutory restrictions on ownership mean that existing organisations will be compelled to sell some of their assets. Not only does this challenge a number of widely held beliefs about the rights of property owners, it also assumes that new entrants to the market, replete with the necessary expertise and capital, can be found. All the evidence suggests this is most unlikely to be the case. Consequently, plurality of supply will ultimately necessitate massive government start-up grants and continuing subsidisation.

The dangers of this – media organisations dependent upon government for their financial existence – have been flagged by each of the three royal commissions on the press called since 1945. The second of these – the Shawcross Commission, 1961–2 - put the case as follows:

> We are all forced to the conclusion – which we regret because of our clear realisation of the dangers that exist – that there is no acceptable legislative or fiscal way of regulating the competitive and economic forces as to ensure . . . sufficient diversity. The only hope of the weaker . . . [organisations] is to secure – as some have done in the past – managers . . . of such enterprise and originality as will enable these [organisations] to overcome the economic forces affecting them. (Quoted in Whale 1980: 39)

As far as UK government is currently concerned, nothing has changed since to invalidate this evaluation.

Conclusion

Quite clearly, government in the UK has consistently rejected intervention in media markets as a means of securing political control, though its motives for doing so and their consequences for the health of the British media remain open to dispute. However, this is not the only option available to ministers seeking to counter the effects of media bias and influence. An alternative lies in the regulation of media content, which duly forms the subject of the next and final chapter.

. . . .

What you should have learnt from reading this chapter

* The very different histories of the print and broadcast media in Britain.

* The dualism in ownership policy and how and why free-market ideas have steadily come to dominate government thinking.

* Why critics of government policy argue for intervention to restrict concentration of ownership and how supporters of the status quo go about rebutting these.

Glossary of key terms

Big Flame The name given to a revolutionary group formed in Liverpool in 1970. (The name itself was taken from the title of a television play about striking workers broadcast the previous year.) Not being a party in the formal sense of the word, 'Big Flame' attempted to stimulate political activity across a wide range of trade union and left-wing organisations over the next decade and a half. It also published an eponymous magazine, which proved influential among those on the political Left concerned over the role played by the media in reinforcing capitalist values. The group eventually ceased to function in 1984. However, a number of its followers took up its critique of the media by helping to secure finance for the short-lived, left-wing national weekly *News on Sunday*.

Bulks Many newspapers are now sold at discounted rates to commercial organisations, most obviously hotels. Though they increase circulation, they do not benefit newspaper revenue to anything like the same extent as individual sales.

Dirigiste A term which refers to a style of politics favouring state control of economic and social activity.

Westminster Hall Parliamentary reform earlier this decade created new arrangements whereby backbench MPs could debate items of interest outside the formal setting of the Commons chamber. The location of these is Westminster Hall, just opposite the Palace of Westminster.

Likely examination questions

In what ways has government policy on media ownership evolved since the Second World War?

What explains the growing influence of neo-liberal ideas over government policy in the broad area of media ownership?

Examine the case for and against government intervention in media markets.

Helpful websites

The Audit Bureau of Circulation – www.abc.org.uk – has a wealth of data on the newspaper industry. Government policy in the area can be accessed via the Department for Culture, Media and Sport at www.culture.gov.uk, whilst Ofcom's role in allocating broadcast licences can be examined in more detail at www.ofcom.org.uk.

Suggestions for further reading

An excellent starting point for a detailed analysis of media ownership policy is John Street's *Mass Media, Politics and Democracy*, especially Chapters 6, 11 and 12. Ownership is also covered in Chapter 4 of Kuhn's *Politics and the Media in Britain* and Chapter 5 of Des Freedman's *The Politics of Media Policy*. As ever, Chapters 23–4 of Curran and Seaton's *Power Without Responsibility* provide a critical and challenging assessment of government thinking.

Media Policy (2): Content

Content

Overview

In the previous chapter we examined media policy as it applies to ownership. Chapter 10 seeks to complete this study of political communication by examining government policy on media content. Though attention will focus on the ways in which governments have sought to regulate content, we will also look at a number of important ancillary issues: notably the implications of constitutional reform for media freedom and the future of the public-service model of British broadcasting as it applies to political reporting.

Key issues to be covered in this chapter

- The case for and against statutory controls on the print media
- The attitude of the courts to the press since the passage of the Human Rights Act
- The rationale behind the regulation of political broadcasting
- The case for a partial deregulation of broadcast coverage of politics

Media freedom and democratic politics

For constitutional liberals, media freedom is 'widely seen as a necessary condition for democracy' (Leach et al. 2006: 151). Some insight into this is provided by Box 10.1. This does not mean that liberal democratic governments are effectively prohibited from restricting media freedoms. Indeed, especially in the age of universal human rights, governments find themselves having to balance the right to publish with other considerations such as privacy. However, whilst the media might be more vulnerable than most to a law of confidence or copyright, this does not imply that they will be deliberately targeted. By contrast, a system of content regulation is designed precisely with the media in mind. Indeed, the key point about content regulation is that it restricts the freedom of the media to publish categories of material which may not be illegal according to the general law. Typical features of a regulatory regime might include:

- A wide-ranging code of conduct.
- A statutory body to monitor this code and enforce agreed standards both prior to and after publication.
- An automatic and extensive right to reply, as a result of which media organisations would be compelled to devote space (or time) to the opinions of a person or group whom they had attacked, allegedly unfairly.
- Fines and other sanctions for journalists who break agreed standards.
- A privacy law placing clear limits on the circumstances in which journalists can legitimately infringe the privacy of individuals and which could be used by the latter to suppress publication and seek damages.
- A bespoke criminal regime punishing the behaviour of individual journalists.

Throughout the twentieth century a system of content regulation has been developing in the UK. However, its individual features are highly sector specific. In part this reflects traditional political attitudes. As we saw in the previous chapter, press freedom has been historically more influential than the complementary idea of freedom for broadcasters. Equally, it reflects political perceptions of

Box 10.1 David Feldman on media freedom

One of the UK's most distinguished writers in this area – David Feldman – has summarised the value of a 'free media' in the following terms:

- Journalists are individuals like any other and, as such, are entitled to regard their ability to write and broadcast freely as a form of self-expression.
- Democratic theory instinctively recognises the importance of voters accessing a plurality of views and opinions, especially where they contradict those of the government. Journalistic freedom plays a vital part in this process.
- Further, the strength of a democratic polity depends upon public awareness of the performance of those in government. However, relatively few people have the time or the resources to conduct their own inquiries. Consequently, voters depend heavily on the ability of journalists to uncover those aspects of public affairs that ministers would prefer to keep hidden.
- In addition, the media play a key part in redressing individual grievances. This is particularly important given the nature of much service delivery. Where market mechanisms do not apply, the media have a key role in ensuring that evidence of poor performance and other failings enters the public domain, whereupon it becomes very difficult for government to ignore.
- However, most importantly, the media can correct the seemingly inevitable human tendencies towards complacency and unjustified respect for ideas and institutions which no longer function as they should. In short, the media has the power to act as a great iconoclast; it can stimulate debate on issues which otherwise powerful forces would prefer to suppress. In short, it can encourage us all to say no to Power.

(*Source:* Feldman 2002: 807)

influence. Whereas press bias is, if not accepted, at least tolerated, the same cannot be said for broadcasters, whose capacity to effect public opinion is believed to be far greater.

This dualism has important implications for the politics of content regulation. The key issue for politicians in respect of the press is the extent to which they should accept the case for a tighter regulatory regime. This is especially so in respect of the right to privacy. With broadcasting, the contours of the debate are very different. Thanks in large part to the persistent lobbying of Rupert Murdoch and News International, the viability of content regulations for broadcasters is increasingly open to question. Murdoch maintains that the BBC has consistently promoted a liberal elitist world view to the detriment of the conservative interest. In other words, the agenda for reform of the rules on broadcasting content points towards deregulation, at least in respect of news reporting. I shall consider both issues in turn.

Regulating the print media

It is easy to see why politicians might be interested in imposing regulations which control media content. Lacking media organisations of their own, regulating content offers them the only direct means of shaping journalistic output. However, following the collapse of the licensing system in the middle of the nineteenth century, government has been particularly wary of tampering with press freedom. One of the few exceptions to this is the reporting of elections, where statute law places small but significant constraints on newspapers. Elsewhere, regulations on newspaper content are notable only by their absence. Consequently, providing they work within the general

---

Box 10.2 Reporting elections

- A general restriction under *s. 75 of the Representation of the People Act 1983 (RPA)* is that newspapers must be careful only to take adverts from authorised sources.
- They are also at risk under the *Defamation Act 1952* in terms of the way they report election addresses.
- However, by far the most important restrictions can be found in *s. 106 of the RPA*. Candidates can obtain an injunction preventing a newspaper from making or repeating a false statement of fact in relation to their conduct or character. Proprietors and editors also commit an offence if, in order to advance the cause of their preferred choices, they publish a false statement that another candidate has withdrawn from the contest.

legal rules in respect of defamation, confidence and so on, the print media are largely free to report as they see fit . . . and to take their chances in court.

The Press Complaints Commission

In terms of regulation, the only measure newspaper owners have been forced to concede is a non-statutory body: the Press Complaints Commission (PCC). The Commission is financed by the industry through a body known as the Press Standards Board of Finance, which, for the record, provides a current budget of £1.9 million per annum. The PCC's origins lie with the now defunct Press Council, established in 1953. However, by the time the last royal commission on the press – the McGregor Commission – reported in 1977, the work of the Press Council was under increasing attack. Whilst

---

Box 10.3 The PCC Code

1. Accuracy – including an obligation to correct inaccurate material
2. Opportunity to reply
3. Privacy – editors must satisfy themselves that breach of privacy can be justified
4. Harassment
5. Special protection from intrusion into grief and shock
6. Special protection for children
7. Special protection for children in sex cases
8. Special protection for medical patients, visitors and hospital staff
9. Special protection for those involved in a criminal investigations
10. Restrictions on the use of covert surveillance
11. Special protection for victims of sexual assault
12. Anti-discrimination provisions
13. Prohibition against the use of information given to journalists for personal financial gain
14. Obligation to protect confidential sources
15. Prohibition against payments to witnesses in criminal cases
16. Prohibition against payments to criminals

(*Source:* Press Complaints Commission)

McGregor rejected calls for a new, statutory system, he was critical of journalistic standards and insisted that the Council be revamped to restore public confidence in the print media.

Calcutt and after

In the following decade, however, complaints about press misconduct continued to grow. The background to this was a combination of declining circulation and intensifying competition, which led to a series of particularly gratuitous media invasions of personal privacy. As a result, the Conservative government appointed David Calcutt to assess the desirability of statutory regulation of the press from without. Calcutt's findings – published as *The Report of the Committee on Privacy and Related Matters in June 1990* – were essentially that the Press Council be scrapped and replaced with a press complaints commission, which would, in turn, establish and enforce a new code of practice. Calcutt added that the new arrangements be given 18 months to demonstrate their worth. However, once it became apparent that the hoped-for improvement in journalistic standards had not materialised, Calcutt was asked to review his findings in a second report, published in January 1993. His conclusions rocked the print media to its core.

- There was little prospect of the PCC bringing about a transformation in press behaviour.
- Consequently, it should be replaced with a statutory regulator with the powers to stop publication of offending material, insist on printed apologies, impose fines on individual journalists for breaching the code of conduct and award financial compensation to victims of press malpractice.
- Specific criminal offences should be created to curb the worst journalistic invasions of privacy.
- A new privacy law should be established to give aggrieved parties an additional means of obtaining redress in the civil courts.

Recognising that it was now in trouble, the press responded by 'beefing up' the PCC's Code. In addition, it embarked on a campaign of intensive lobbying, systematically rebutting Calcutt in a 'White Paper' entitled *Media Freedom and Media Regulation*. A digest of these arguments, which includes additional points made subsequently by the PCC itself, is set out below:

- Unlike a statutory regulator, the PCC is entirely compatible with the tradition of press freedom.
- Newspapers are much more likely to take notice of and cooperate with a body over which they have a degree of influence and, more importantly, which they perceive to be knowledgeable about their own needs and circumstances.
- Despite the criticisms listed above, the PCC's efforts are beginning to pay off (Table 10.1). In addition, the PCC can refer to a variety of qualitative data: the fact that individual contracts of employment are now inserting clauses enabling editors to be dismissed for breach of the Code and the growing tendency of the press (and even broadcasters) to consult it prior to publication being two of the most important.
- It is also contended that those who favour a statutory scheme ignore the practical advantages of the PCC's Code in two important respects: it is flexible and cheap to use. None of these would apply to a statutory regulator with the powers to stop publication and issue fines, since the latter's decisions would be routinely challenged in court with all this implies for the speed and cost of obtaining justice.
- The intellectual case for new and sweeping primary legislation in respect of new criminal offences and a formal law of privacy has not been made across the full range of privacy issues. This is especially so in light of numerous statutes which already exist to restrain journalistic practices: the 'White Paper' cited 46 of these, though this figure is now almost certainly higher.

As suggested above, the press can draw heavily on the findings of the McGregor Commission. In a significant blow to the case for statutory regulation and a new regime of criminal offences, McGregor insisted that, as a matter of principle, the press should stand before the same law as any other organisation or individual. More importantly still, McGregor also argued that meaningful statutory regulation necessitated extensive pre-publication monitoring, the interference with property rights and imposition of sanctions, all of which would compromise press freedoms. Modern parlance refers to 'a chilling effect'. This is a strong restatement of classical liberalism. However, it is worth adding that McGregor was under no

Table 10.1 Handling complaints: the PCC and Ofcom (2008)

	Complaints received	Rulings made	Complaints resolved
Ofcom	67,742	12,532	25
PCC	4,698	1,420	550

(*Source:* Gore and Horgan 2009)

illusions about the unsatisfactory nature of much press reporting. It was simply that, in his eyes, to take responsibility for fixing this away from proprietors and editors was to pay too high a price for what was otherwise a desirable purchase (Whale 1980: 156–7).

The 1995 White Paper and after

The Major government's response was long delayed. Indeed it was not until 1995 that the government published a White Paper setting out its views. These rejected all of Calcutt's main demands. Though there was some intellectual justification for this decision, Kuhn (2007: 137–8) argues that the government's reticence reflected ministerial fears of a press backlash: 'The certainty of the whole press . . . mobilising against the proposed legislation on statutory regulation can be reasonably expected to have weighed in the balance of ministerial calculations'.

The Blair and Brown governments have both fallen in behind this policy. The net effect is that, despite continued reservations over the PCC, the prospect of a statutory regime is now remote. Instead, attention has focused on the prospect of tougher criminal sanctions for journalists for illegally obtaining personal data. This issue has become particularly prominent in the aftermath of the **Goodman case** (see the glossary at the end of this chapter). Former Information Commissioner Richard Thomas has voiced his fears that a black market in personal information is booming in the UK, centring on journalists' routine use of private detectives to search for such information. Thomas felt sufficiently strongly about this as to compile and publish a 'league table', the *Daily Mail* topping it with 982 pieces of information paid for by no fewer than 60 of its journalists. Without suggesting that such practices are intrinsically illegal or

Box 10.4 Investigative journalism and the criminal law: the key offences

Protection from Harassment Act 1997

- This statute, popularly described as an 'anti-stalking measure', was originally passed to help private citizens protect themselves against stalkers. Under ss. 1 and 4 it is possible to obtain a court order banning a named individual from approaching or otherwise contacting another person. Breach of such an order carries a maximum sentence of five years in custody.

Regulation of Investigatory Powers Act 2000

- It is an offence under s. 1(1)–(2) to unlawfully intercept the communications of another, punishable on indictment by a maximum sentence of two years and an unlimited fine
- The unlawful acquisition and disclosure of communications data (for example, websites visited by an internet browser) is a civil offence, for which the aggrieved party will seek large financial damages.

Data Protection Act 1998

- Under s. 55(3) it is an offence to obtain or disclose personal data or information without the consent of the data controller. However, there is an important public interest defence to this offence. Further, even if found guilty, the worst punishment a journalist can receive is an unlimited fine.

even unethical, they do point to a 'broader picture, where dirty tricks and illegal activity still appear to be seen by some journalists as part of their professional toolkit' (Gibson 2007). In 2007, lobbying by the Information Commissioner's Office (ICO) appeared to have paid off when it obtained government approval for an amendment to s. 55 of the Data Protection Act which would have made obtaining and disclosing personal data an imprisonable offence (Davies 2009). However, after facing intensive pressure from the newspaper industry, in April 2008 the government once again backed away from confrontation and withdrew its own proposals, much to the exasperation of both Thomas and his successor (Leigh and Evans 2008).

A 'back door' privacy law?

However, despite the government's unwillingness to formally tackle what many continue to be seen as predatory and unscrupulous practices within the print media, leading industry representatives insist that their freedoms are nevertheless facing an unprecedented threat. 'There is one remaining threat to press freedom that . . . may prove far more dangerous to . . . [the newspaper] industry . . . Inexorably, and insidiously, the British press is having a privacy law imposed upon it' (Dacre 2008).

For many decades the courts have been developing bodies of law which protect the individual from the consequences of inaccurate reporting (defamation) and intrusive investigative methods (confidence). Though much attention has been given to the law of defamation (Monbiot 2008; Hanson 2009), the concern of Dacre and his colleagues in the Society of Editors lies with a series of legal rulings which have extended the historic law of confidence in ways 'which – apart from allowing the corrupt and crooked to sleep easily in their beds – . . . [are] undermining the ability of mass-circulation newspapers to sell newspapers in an ever more difficult market'.

The rationale behind the law of confidence was summed up by J. Meggary in *Coco* v. *A. N. Clark (Engineers) Ltd* (1968) when he described confidence as the cousin of trust, adding that without it all personal and commercial life becomes impossible. Few would disagree. However, the print media argued that this principle had to be balanced against the fact that the press's ability to uncover wrongdoing in the public interest invariably involves serious breaches of confidence – whether through subterfuge such as the '**fake sheikh**' affair, long-range photography or buying personal information from 'insider' sources. The courts accepted this and allowed what is known as the public interest defence. This did not mean that the media was able to assume that whatever is of interest to the public is in the public interest. In particular, the courts insisted that the information provided had to be new and useful, rather than prurient or appealing to morbid curiosity. So, for example, the courts allowed the press to breach confidence providing that it could show, as per Lord Denning's ruling in *Woodward* v. *Hutchins* (1977), that the gravity of the story merited publication regardless of the seriousness of the breach. Alternatively, where it was established that the complainant has benefited from living in the public's eye, the courts might decide to reduce the level of protection offered – Lord Woolf in *A* v. *B plc* (2002). In this way a balance was struck. This did not mean that the print media always approved judicial rulings. However, there was no sense that newspapers were so aggrieved that they felt the need to lobby for a change in the law.

Dacre's concern is that, following the implementation of the 1998 Human Rights Act, this balance has been disturbed. The cases at the centre of the dispute are listed in Box 10.5. However, whilst Dacre is highly critical of the judge at the centre of the controversy – Mr Justice Eady – he reserves most of his fire for the government: 'If (Prime Minister Gordon) Brown wanted to force a privacy law, he would have set out a bill, arguing the case in both houses of parliament, withstand public scrutiny and win [sic] a series of votes'.

The implication is clear. Rather than formally reopen the debate initiated by Calcutt in 1993, New Labour is seeking instead to muzzle the media indirectly through the work of Mr Justice Eady and the Human Rights Act. This is a strong accusation and immediately recalls the media's initial response to the second Calcutt report: to the effect that the political class is seeking to use a general law for its private benefit. However, as Dacre points out, the stakes are high. In particular, he links the effective collapse of the best-selling newspaper market in France to draconian privacy laws which prevent its press from publishing sensational exposés of leading celebrities. Dacre is in no doubt that the best-selling UK dailies and weeklies would not survive in their present form if denied the capacity to print this type of article by the courts. If so, one might safely suggest that this aspect of the debate on content regulation is set to run and run for some time yet.

Broadcasting: state-imposed impartiality

In keeping with the dualism apparent in government policy on ownership, politicians have once again adopted a very different approach to broadcasting content. As Robertson and Nicol note: 'Television and radio are subject to much more stringent laws and regulatory systems than apply to the press'. They add that official circles

Box 10.5 A 'back door' privacy law: the key cases

The Prince's diaries
On 21 December 2006, the Court of Appeal ruled in a case where the Prince of Wales had sued the *Mail on Sunday* for breach of confidence and copyright when it published extracts from one of eight diaries handed to the paper by a former employee without his consent. Significantly, the court ruled that neither the gravity of the story, the Prince's highly public persona nor the fact that he had made the diaries available to his friends outweighed his right to privacy as set out in Article 8(1) of the European Convention of Human Rights.

The unauthorised biography of Loreena McKennitt
Shortly before this, the same court ruled in an even more important case brought by the Canadian singer Loreena McKennitt. The issue involved the right of her former aide, Neima Ash, to include personal information about the singer in her unauthorised biography of McKennitt's life. By finding for Ms McKennitt, the court called into question the media's ability to use information supplied by well-placed insiders – the so-called 'kiss and tell' stories – in their revelations about the rich and famous. This applies even when the latter had used the media to tell their own version of their stories on previous occasions. The likely effect on the tabloids was described as 'dramatic' (Dyer 2006).

The unconventional life of Max Mosley
This was a sordid case which attracted international media attention. On 24 July 2008, Mosley won his action for breach of confidence against the *News of the World* and was awarded a record payout – £60,000 – in a case of this type. In a statement which no doubt chilled the hearts of the press, Mr Justice Eady recorded that neither Mosley's high public profile nor the distasteful nature of his conduct justified such an extensive invasion of his privacy in light of – and this is the key point – a 'modern rights-based jurisprudence'. Eady went on to add that 'there was no public interest or other justification for the clandestine recording, for the publication of the resulting information and still photographs, or for the placing of the video extracts on the *News of the World* website – all of this on a massive scale' (quoted in Holmwood and Fitzsimmons 2008). In other words, the gravity of the story was simply not great enough to justify the methods the paper used to obtain it.

Box 10.6 Taking political control of broadcasting content

- Under *para. 81(2) of the BBC Agreement* the Secretary of State can, in an emergency situation, order the BBC to broadcast any announcement or programme, effectively taking control of the Corporation.
- Under *para. 81(1) and (4)* of the same document, a minister can order the BBC to carry an announcement or direct it not to broadcast any specified matter or class of matter. These powers can be used in non-emergency situations.
- A parallel power which applies to commercial broadcasters is contained in s. *10(3) of the 1990 Broadcasting Act.*

continue to view television in particular as a guest in the home, 'one which must be carefully groomed and programmed before being allowed to visit' (2002: 272–3). Politicians have proved particularly sensitive to this and, as we shall now see, have taken appropriate steps to ensure that they do not become victims of partial coverage.

The broadcast codes

The more draconian powers available to ministers are set out in Box 10.6. However, the fact that these provisions are used very rarely has tended to focus attention on the codes of conduct which form the core of the system of broadcast content control. These work in rather different ways. Content regulation of the BBC is achieved via its Charter. This ensures that the BBC exists to serve the public interest, which it does in the main by promoting a number of public purposes. These are set in paragraph 4 and include: sustaining citizenship and civil society; promoting education and learning; stimulating creativity and cultural excellence; representing the UK's nations, regions and communities; and bringing the UK to the world and vice versa. In addition, the BBC's Agreement stipulates that the overarching content of the BBC's UK Public Services must be: of high quality; challenging; original; and both innovative and engaging. Every item it broadcasts must exhibit at least one of these characteristics. These are supported by a variety of rules set out elsewhere in the Agreement which producers must follow.

Very similar arrangements apply to the commercial sector, where responsibility for enforcing content controls lies with the statutory regulator, Ofcom. In addition to allocating licences, Ofcom is obliged under s. 319 of the 2003 Communications Act to set standards for programming in the form of a Broadcasting Code. In turn, the Code must aim to meet six statutory objectives:

- The protection of those aged under eighteen
- The exclusion of material which is likely to encourage crime or disorder
- The presentation of news with due impartiality
- The reporting of news with due accuracy
- Ensuring that religious affairs programming is undertaken with the appropriate degree of responsibility
- The protection of the public from harmful and offensive material.

Political reporting: the concept of due impartiality
Governments have worked hard to ensure that these arrangements include measures to control political reporting. The following account is based on the Ofcom Code, though the BBC's own regulations under paragraphs 44 and 47 of its Agreement are virtually identical.

Where an item falls into one of the following categories – political or industrial controversy or a matter relating to current public policy – it is covered by the special impartiality requirements. Essentially, these are designed to prevent:

- The person providing the news service from expressing their own views on the matter being reported. (Where a person presenting a news item is known to have a personal view, this must be made known to the audience and appropriate provision made for the expression of alternatives.)
- Only certain viewpoints being expressed (due impartiality).

The Ofcom Code provides further amplification of the meaning of the term 'due impartiality'. What it does not mean is that every possible argument has to be represented, or that an equal weight must be given to every possible viewpoint or perspective. Instead, the item being covered must be given its 'due' balance. Viewpoints which appear to run counter to generally accepted standards can be ignored altogether.

The most important feature of the special impartiality requirements is that they apply not just to news programmes. In addition, where the item is a 'major' political or industrial controversy or matter of current policy, the requirement of impartiality refers to each programme, or a clearly linked number of programmes. Further, these impartiality rules are reinforced by a complex system of internal and external complaints. As we have seen, this has proved of particular value to spin doctors who routinely use it to apply moral pressure on broadcasters in respect of their choice and presentation of news items.

The political value of content regulation

Whilst the parties might gain a general satisfaction from knowing that broadcasters labour under the weight of regulation, the extent to which they afford a distinct advantage to individual parties is questionable. Most obviously, the privileges available to one are available to all. Consequently, whilst the parties can insist on impartial coverage, this is something of a double-edged weapon: the other side can insist on exactly the same right. Secondly, they provide parties with every incentive to continuously monitor broadcasting output. As a result, the machinations of one party will be closely watched by others. Any suggestion that broadcasters are capitulating to undue pressure will elicit a response and, no doubt, a string of complaints.

Similarly, ministers seeking to use the provisions listed in Box 10.6 above will be only too aware that they contain powers which cannot be overused. The power to order the BBC and Ofcom to block the transmission of a programme is a wide-ranging one, but runs the risk of passive resistance by broadcast executives who might use their discretion to inform their audiences of ministerial directives. This will be taken up by other sections of the media, who will no doubt 'frame' it in ways designed to exploit still further popular cynicism towards the UK's political elite.

Due impartiality: the case for reform

The argument in favour of content control dates from the very inception of broadcasting, in particular 'that television is a uniquely powerful and persuasive medium' (Robertson and Nicol 2007: 912). However, in recent times more voices have been heard questioning the legitimacy of this view. One reason for this is that the advent of narrowcasting and the internet has freed the public from its dependence on the four main free-to-air broadcasters and enables it to obtain its news and current affairs content from an unprecedented range of media. In such circumstances, partiality in television news coverage loses its sting. Secondly, and more seriously, it is argued that the concept of due impartiality has shackled the creativity of broadcast journalism. Robertson and Nicol (2007: 912) make this point with characteristic terseness when they note that 'Television's contribution to public affairs is lacklustre, in terms of exposure journalism and agenda setting, and its executives are cautious and conventional'. This criticism is particularly relevant to the coverage of elections, where dull broadcasting content has been linked to low levels of engagement and poor turnout. The implication is that broadcasters are simply too mindful of their exposure to complaints of partiality and unfairness and, rather than opt for hard-hitting programming which offers an audience a consistent if partial account, prefer a more anodyne treatment which nonetheless ensures that all the main viewpoints are aired within a single transmission. This type of critic can point out that the original 'due impartiality' provision was very much the work of Margaret Thatcher who was determined to check what she believed to be an anti-Conservative bias among broadcasters. In other words, if due impartiality has contributed to the chilling effect on journalism, then it has done precisely what was intended for it.

Professor Franklin offers an alternative, albeit oblique, criticism of government policy on political reporting. This focuses less on the consequences of the regulations than on those emanating from the manipulation of the market conditions under which broadcasters operate. This has been felt much more by the commercial sector than the BBC. He argues that the neo-liberal influences in broadcast legislation from 1986 to 2003 have placed considerable constraints 'on programme range and quality'. The ITV regional franchises, ITN and Channel 4 have felt these particularly keenly, leading Franklin (2004: 36) to suggest that the denial of economic resources has been a deliberate ploy to reduce the amount of documentary and current affairs programming on television: 'They (politicians) know . . . that market forces limit broadcasters' choices in predictable ways. The "invisible hand" of the market placed across a broadcaster's mouth can gag as effectively as any censor.'

It has long been suggested that governments have a vested interest in steering broadcasters away from 'hard' news programming in favour of 'light' entertainment. The emphasis on market forces as a key instrument of broadcasting policy assists in this, largely by fueling the ratings war. Programme-makers come under renewed pressure to make programmes that are 'popular' rather than investing resources in programmes which audiences may watch but turn away advertisers. In this way, the state-funded BBC is caught up in the process of commercialisation. Its ability to secure public finance increasingly depends upon demonstrating to ministers the relevance of its programming to a mass audience. As a result, the comments of US broadcasters on the limited arrival of commercial television in 1955 seem to have lost nothing of their relevance: 'Dear Little John Bulls / Don't you cry, / You'll soon be full commercial / Bye and bye.'

Plurality in a new media age

However, the argument currently gaining political momentum is very much the work of the political Right. We have seen on numerous occasions throughout the latter part of this study how and why conservative commentators argue that the rules on impartiality have effectively broken down because of a failure of BBC managers to correct a pronounced left-wing bias within the corporation's journalism. These will not repay repetition here. What is significant, however, is the extent to which this critique may influence the policy of a future Conservative government. The first real sign that the Conservatives might break with the cross-party consensus on the broadcast codes came in April 2008, when the Conservative Research Department (CRD) published a discussion document entitled *Plurality in a New Media Age*. The key passages can be found on pages 14–16, where the CRD quotes at length the fears of BBC insiders that the Corporation may be routinely failing to meet its obligations under due impartiality. One means of correcting this is to free those broadcasters not in receipt of public funding from the obligation to report the news impartially. The Conservatives argue that this will encourage newspapers to enter broadcast markets by establishing their own digital channels or internet TV services. However, critics point out that the principal beneficiary will be Rupert Murdoch, who will get his wish to transform Sky News into the UK equivalent of his overtly pro-conservative Fox News, which currently broadcasts in the US. What interesting times that would make for practitioners and students of political communication!

Afterword

This chapter has tried to demonstrate two things. Firstly, that the debate on regulating media content is very much alive. Secondly, that the development of a neo-conservative agenda on broadcasting content could have significant consequences for political communication. In doing so it reminds us of the dynamic nature of modern (or should that be post-modern?) political communication and how the latter is continually changing our understanding of contemporary politics. This, in reality, has been the leitmotif of this book. Quite simply, whether you are studying party ideology and organisation, the nature of the core executive, the action and influence of pressure groups, the strength of the UK or one of a hundred or more other subjects besides, don't ignore the significance and impact of political communication. This is one area of the public domain where politics really do matter.

· ·

✅ What you should have learnt from reading this chapter

- The reasons why the media has a critical part to play in the proper functioning of a liberal democracy.

- How the tradition of a 'free press' has influenced public policy.

- Why the print media are so concerned about a legal threat to their commercial interests.

- The nature and impact of content regulations on the broadcast media.

- Why many commentators now argue that these regulations should be relaxed.

Glossary of key terms

'Fake sheikh' This refers to the now infamous 'sting' orchestrated by the *News of the World* in which the then manager of the English national soccer team, Sven Goran-Eriksson, was tricked into making highly embarrassing revelations by a man (the 'fake sheikh') he believed might be a future employer. The whole episode hastened Eriksson's departure from his post, as a result of which he threatened to sue the paper for breach of confidence and privacy.

Goodman case Aside from the fact that the fears of breaching the Code failed to have any discernible impact on Goodman's conduct, the real story was in the alleged failure of the PCC to properly question his employers – News International – in order to uncover whether paying for illegal interception of communications was widespread. The fact that the PCC found in favour of News International was later a source of embarrassment when *The Guardian* subsequently published materials suggesting such illegality was routine at the *News of the World* and that the only reason why more journalists had escaped prosecution was because of the newspaper's policy of 'buying off' victims.

Likely examination questions

Explain the political importance of media freedom in a liberal democratic state.

To what extent is it still correct to talk of a 'free press' in the UK?

Critically assess the case for abolishing the regulations on 'due impartiality' as they currently apply to the broadcast media.

Helpful websites

The work of the Press Complaints Commission can be explored in more detail at www.pcc.org.uk. This includes information on the PCC Code and the complaints process. Anyone seeking to examine the broadcast codes and the complaints system should refer to www.bbc.co.uk/info and go to 'About us'. Similarly, the Ofcom Broadcasting Code can be found at www.ofcom.org.uk/tv/ifi/codes/bcode. The media's view on a range of regulatory issues is available on the Society of Editors website: www.societyofeditors.co.uk.

Suggestions for further reading

Further coverage of the history of content regulation and the ensuing debates can be found in Chapter 5 of Kuhn's *Politics and the Media in Britain* and Chapter 6 of Des Freedman's *The Politics of Media Policy*

(Cambridge: Polity, 2008). Chapters 5, 14 and 16 of Robertson and Nicol's *Media Law* provide a very detailed explanation of the law as it applies to media content. An excellent PCC paper setting out the case for voluntary regulation – 'Maintaining Freedom and Responsibility', by William Gore and John Horgan – can be found at www.pcc.org.uk/news. The CRD paper *Plurality in a New Media Age* is available at www.conservatives.com.

References

Allen, N. (2006), 'A Restless Electorate: Stirrings in the Political Season', in J. Bartle and A. King (eds), *Britain at the Polls* (Washington, DC: CQ Press).

Ballinger, C. (2002), 'The Local Battle, the Cyber Battle', in D. Butler and D. Kavanagh, *The British General Election 2001* (Basingstoke: Palgrave).

Bartle, J. (2006), 'The Labour Government and the Media', in J. Bartle and A. King (eds), *Britain at the Polls* (Washington, DC: CQ Press).

Baston, L. (2001), 'The Party System', in A. Seldon (ed.), *The Blair Effect* (London: Little, Brown).

Blair, T. (2007), 'Lecture by the Prime Minister the Right Honourable Tony Blair MP on Public Life', 10 Downing Street Press Notice, 12 June.

Blumler, J. G and M. Gurevitch (1995), *The Crisis of Political Communication* (London: Routledge).

Blumler and D. McQuail (1968), *Television in Politics* (London: Faber).

Branigan, T. (2006), 'Primary colours', *Guardian*, 19 April.

Budge, I., D. McKay, J. Bartle and K. Newton (2007), *The New British Politics* (Harlow: Pearson).

Butler, D. (1995), *British General Elections since 1945* (Oxford: Blackwell).

Butler, D. and D. Kavanagh (1992), *The British General Election 1992* (Basingstoke: Macmillan).

Butler, D. and D. Kavanagh (1997), *The British General Election 1997* (Basingstoke: Macmillan).

Butler, D. and D. Kavanagh (2002), *The British General Election 2001* (Basingstoke: Palgrave).

Butler, D. and D. Kavanagh (2006), *The British General Election 2005* (Basingstoke: Palgrave).

Colville (2008), *Politics, Policy and the Internet*, www.cps.org.uk.

Coughlan, S. (2001), 'First Time Voters Ignored Election', http://news.bbc.co.uk/1/hi/education/2966275.stm.

Crockett, R. (1994), 'The Party, Publicity and the Media', in A. Seldon and S. Ball (eds), *The Conservative Century* (Oxford: Oxford University Press).

Curran, J and J. Seaton (2003), *Power Without Responsibility* (London: Routledge).

Curtice, J and M. Steed (1997), 'The Results Analysed', in D. Butler and D. Kavanagh, *The British General Election 1997* (Basingstoke: Macmillan).

Dacre, P. (2007), 'The BBC's cultural Marxism will trigger an American-style backlash', *Guardian*, 24 January.

Dacre, P. (2008), 'The threat to our press', *Guardian*, 10 November.

Dale, I. (2009), 'Labour listing', *Guardian*, 12 January.

Davies, N. (2006), *Flat Earth News* (London: Chatto and Windus).

Davies, N. (2009), 'The law on phone hacking', *Guardian*, 8 July.

Denver, D. (2007), *Elections and Voting Behaviour in Britain* (Basingstoke: Palgrave Macmillan).

Dyer, C. (2006), 'Landmark ruling could spell end of "kiss and tell"', *Guardian*, 15 December.

Faucher-King, F. (2009), 'The Party is Over: the "Modernization" of the British Labour Party', in T. Casey (ed.), *The Blair Legacy* (Basingstoke: Palgrave Macmillan).

Feldman, D. (2002), *Civil Liberties and Human Rights in England and Wales* (Oxford: Oxford University Press).

Fisher, J., D. Denver, E. Fieldhouse, D. Cutts and A. Russell (2005), *Constituency Campaigning in the 2005 General Election*, www.essex.ac.uk/.../EPOP%20 for%20Fisher%20et20al.doc.

Foster, S. (1994), *Political Parties* (Sheffield: PAVIC/Politics Association).

Foster, S. (1999), 'Law and Order', in R. Kelly (ed.), *Changing Party Policy in Britain* (Oxford: Blackwell).

Franklin, B. (1997), *Newszak and News Media* (London: Arnold).

Franklin, B. (2004), *Packaging Politics* (London: Hodder Arnold).

Freedman, D. (2008), *The Politics of Media Policy* (Cambridge: Polity).

Gardner, J. (2006), 'The GOP Voter Vault's Data Resources put the FBI, NSA, and Santa Claus to Shame', http://blogcritics.org/politics/ article/the-gop-voter-vaults-data-resources, 1 November.

Garton-Ash, T. (2004), 'Europe's shape must not be dictated by unelected newspaper proprietors', *Guardian*, 5 April.

Gibson, O. (2007a), 'Internal report attacks BBC liberal consensus', *Guardian*, 19 June.

Gibson, O. (2007b), 'Code breaker', *Guardian*, 29 January.

Gore and Horgan (2009), *Maintaining freedom and responsibility*, www.pcc.org. uk/news.

Gould, P. (1998), *The Unfinished Revolution* (London: Little, Brown).

Hanson, N. (2009), 'Review of internet libel law is overdue', www.society-ofeditors.co.uk, 22 September.

Hencke, D. (2008), 'Top Tories told to name rich donors funding private offices', *Guardian*, 26 April.

Hernan, E. S and N. Chomsky (1988), *Manufacturing Consent* (New York: Pantheon).

Hinsliff, G. (2008), 'Labour heads for financial collapse', *Observer*, 22 June.

Holmwood, L. and C. Fitzsimmons (2008), 'Max Mosley wins £60,000 in privacy case', *www.guardian.co.uk*, 24 July.

Jones, B. (2006), 'The Mass Media and Political Communication', in B. Jones, D. Kavanagh, M. Moran and P. Norton, *Politics UK* (Harlow: Pearson).

Jones, N. (2007), 'How Blair rewrote the media rule book', *Guardian*, 14 May.

Jones, S., O. Gibson and S. Brook (2008), 'It's the Standard wot won it', *Guardian*, 3 May.

Kettle, M. (2008), 'Actually, it wasn't the *Sun* wot won it. *Sun* readers did', *Guardian*, 7 June.

Kavanagh, D. (1995), *Election Campaigning* (Oxford: Blackwell).

King, A. (2006), 'Why Labour Won – Yet Again', in J. Bartle and A. King (eds), *Britain at the Polls* (Washington, DC: CQ Press).

Kuhn, R. (2005), 'Media Management', in A. Seldon, and D. Kavanagh (eds), *The Blair Effect 2001–5* (Cambridge: Cambridge University Press), 2005, pp. 94–111.

Kuhn, R. (2007), *Politics and the Media in Britain* (Basingstoke: Palgrave Macmillan).

Lazarsfeld, P., B. Berelson and H. Gaudet [1944] (1988) (3rd edn), *The People's Choice* (New York: Columbia University Press).

Leach, R., B. Coxall and L. Robins (2006), *British Politics* (Basingstoke: Palgrave Macmillan).

Leigh, D., R. Norton-Taylor and R. Evans (2007), 'MI6 and Blair at odds over Saudi deals', *Guardian*, 16 January.

Leigh, D. and R. Evans (2008), 'PM seeks retreat on bill to outlaw press spying', *Guardian*, 1 April.

Lees-Marshment, J. (2001), *Political Marketing and British Political Parties: the Party's Just Begun* (Manchester: Manchester University Press).

Lees-Marshment, J. and J. Roberts (2005), 'Why it Didn't Work for Labour', paper published by the Chartered Institute of Marketing, UK, see www.

cim.co.uk/mediastore/Election_2005/Election_2005_-_Why_it_did_ not_work_for_Labour_article.pdf.

Linton, M. (1995), 'Sun powered politics', *Guardian*, 30 October.

Lloyd, J. (2004), *What the Media are Doing to Our Politics* (London: Constable).

McCormick, A. (2009), 'The man behind Obama', http://revolutionmaga-zine.com/news/search/903724/man-behind-Obama.

McElhatton, N. (2008), 'UK politicians "need to learn the digital lessons of the US presidential election"', www.marketingdirect mag.co.uk/ news/858943/UK-politicians-need-learn-digital.

McNair, B. (2007), *An Introduction to Political Communication* (Oxford: Routledge).

Miller, W. (1991), *Media and Voters* (Oxford: Oxford University Press).

Monbiot, G. (2008), 'A national disgrace, a global menace and a pre-democratic anachronism', *Guardian*, 15 July.

Murphy, J. (2009), 'No 10 turns to Alastair Campbell and Gould to advise inexperienced election team', *London Evening Standard*, 14 September.

Negrine, R. (1994), *Politics and the Mass Media in Britain* (Abingdon: Routledge).

Newton, K. and M. Brynin (2001), 'The National Press and Party Voting in the UK', *Political Studies*, 49: 265–84.

Norris, P. (1997), 'Political Communication', in P. Dunleavy et al. (eds), *Developments in British Politics 5* (Basingstoke: Macmillan).

Norris, P., J. Curtice, D. Sanders, M. Scammell and H. Semetko (1999), *On Message: Communicating the Campaign* (London: Sage).

Oborne, P. and S. Walters (2004), *Alastair Campbell* (London: Aurum Press).

Price, L. (2006), 'Rupert Murdoch is effectively a member of Blair's Cabinet', *Guardian*, 1 July.

Robertson, G. and A. Nicol (2008), *Media Law* (London: Penguin).

Rosenbaum, M. (1997), *From Soapbox to Soundbite* (Basingstoke: Macmillan).

Sarachan, S. (2009), 'Harnessing the Power of the Social Media: Understanding the Strategy and Impact of the Obama campaign in Digital Public Relations', http://blogarchive.hillandknowlton.com/ blogs/ampersand/articles/11677.aspx.

Scammell, M. (2001), 'Media and Media Management', in A. Seldon (ed.), *The Blair Effect* (London: Little, Brown).

Sheerin, M. (2009), 'March ABCs: more gloom in Scotland', www.pressga-zette.co.uk, 9 April.

Silver, J. (2007), 'Will Gordon stop the spin?', *Guardian*, 18 June.

Sparrow, A. (2009), 'How Derek Draper's plans for an anti-Tory gossip website went awry', *Guardian*, 15 April.

Stevenson, N. (1995), *Understanding Media Cultures* (London: Sage).

Street, J. (2001), *Mass Media, Politics and Democracy* (Basingstoke: Palgrave).

Thompson, J. (1988), 'Mass Communication and Modern Culture: Contribution to a Critical Theory of Ideology', *Sociology* 22(3), 359–83.

Toynbee, P. (2007), 'Our press, the worst in the west, demoralises us all', *Guardian*, 13 April.

Trenaman, J. and D. McQuail (1961), *Television and the Political Image* (London: Methuan).

Watt, N. and J. Borger (2004), 'Tories reveal secret weapon to target voters', *Guardian*, 9 October.

Whale (1980), *Politics of the Media* (London: Fontana).

Wheatcroft, G. (2007), 'Alas, Alastair, if only you'd heeded your own advice', *Guardian*, 7 August.

Wilby, P. (2008), 'The wrong scapegoats', *Guardian*, 20 October.

Wintour, P., V. Dodd and W. Woodward (2006), 'Police quiz Blair inside Downing Street on peerages', *Guardian*, 15 December.

Woodward, W. (2008), 'Cameron tells Ashcroft to clarify his tax position', *Guardian*, 11 February.

Wring, D. (2005), *The Marketing of Labour* (Basingstoke: Palgrave Macmillan).

Wring, D. (2006), 'The News Media and the Public Relations State', in P. Dunleavy et al. (eds), *Developments in British Politics 8* (Basingstoke: Palgrave).

Index

Bold indicates that the term is defined